职业教育经济管理类"十四五"系列教材

商务英语写作

主　编　熊有生　熊婧程　周　祥
副主编　汤素娜　闫　娟　韩　昱　史艳华
参　编　梁乐坤　廖素清　陈　婷　谢凤娇
　　　　王　蔚　张剑斌　朱加宝

华中科技大学出版社
http://press.hust.edu.cn
中国·武汉

内 容 提 要

"商务英语写作"是一门专注于培养学生在商务环境中进行书面沟通能力的课程,其教学内容丰富,旨在使学生掌握在商务场合中有效使用英语进行书面交流的技能。本教材有机融合各类商务文书的基本概念、功能、分类、写作技巧等,强调了商务沟通中的简明性、准确性、专业性以及礼貌性。本教材涵盖求学求职类文书、办公事务类文书、宣传广告类文书、商务礼仪类信函、商务报告建议类文书等五大模块,共计22个写作任务,详细阐述了各类商务文书的格式、结构、常用表达等,提供了大量实用的例句和范文。选材兼具广度与深度,在确保满足高职学生能力需求的基础上,力求考虑学生专升本、海外留学等现实需求。值得一提的是,本教材还穿插介绍了商务沟通中的礼仪和文化差异等内容,以帮助学生更好地适应不同商务环境中的沟通需求。同时,本教材还提供了丰富的写作练习和案例,以便学生进行实践操作和巩固所学知识。总的来说,《商务英语写作》内容全面、实用,旨在通过系统的学习和实践,提升学生的商务英语写作能力,为他们未来顺利应对职场挑战打下坚实的基础。

图书在版编目(CIP)数据

商务英语写作/熊有生,熊婧程,周祥主编. -- 武汉:华中科技大学出版社,2024.10. -- ISBN 978-7-5772-0993-7

Ⅰ. F7

中国国家版本馆CIP数据核字第2024U0G203号

商务英语写作
Shangwu Yingyu Xiezuo

熊有生 熊婧程 周 祥 主编

策划编辑:聂亚文
责任编辑:江旭玉
封面设计:孢　子
责任校对:张汇娟
责任监印:周治超

出版发行:华中科技大学出版社(中国·武汉)　　电话:(027)81321913
　　　　　武汉市东湖新技术开发区华工科技园　　邮编:430223

录　　排:孙雅丽
印　　刷:武汉科源印刷设计有限公司
开　　本:787mm×1092mm　1/16
印　　张:14.25
字　　数:400千字
版　　次:2024年10月第1版第1次印刷
定　　价:48.00元

本书若有印装质量问题,请向出版社营销中心调换
全国免费服务热线:400-6679-118　竭诚为您服务
版权所有　侵权必究

编 委 会

主编
熊有生：广州铁路职业技术学院
熊婧程：莫纳什大学（Monash University）
周　祥：广东工程职业技术学院

副主编
汤素娜：广东行政职业学院
闫　娟：广州铁路职业技术学院
韩　昱：广州铁路职业技术学院
史艳华：广州铁路职业技术学院

参编人员
梁乐坤：广州铁路职业技术学院
廖素清：广州铁路职业技术学院
陈　婷：广州铁路职业技术学院
谢凤娇：广州铁路职业技术学院
王　蔚：广州铁路职业技术学院
张剑斌：广州联强信息技术有限公司
朱加宝：华南电商产业科技（深圳）有限公司

前 言

  随着中国对外开放的规模和深度日益扩大,对外经济贸易业务也日趋依赖素质不断提高的外语人才。作为培养学生对外商务活动核心技能的商务英语写作课程,如何适应新形势、新特点与新要求,正是本书关注的焦点之一。

  全书由求学求职类文书、办公事务类文书、宣传广告类文书、商务礼仪类信函、商务报告建议类文书五大模块组成,每个模块均包含若干个写作任务。全书在选材方面兼具广度与深度,在确保满足高职学生能力需求的基础上,还力求考虑学生专升本、海外留学等现实需求。

  本书以工作过程系统化课程开发理念为指导,将理论与实践紧密联系,力求培养学生的专业素养和实践能力,充分体现培养具备高素质技术技能的商务英语专业人才的要求。

  本书各模块主要由学习目标、任务情景、引导问题、理论介绍、经典范文、结构分析、写作指导、常用句型、问题解答、写作实训等部分组成。

  本书具有如下特点。

  一是情景性。本书内容组织以李梅(Mable)在现实职场中遇到的写作任务情景为主线,写作任务的难度随李梅能力及职位上升而依次递增。

  二是实用性。本书中的任务安排、案例选取、教学实施、考核评价等,按照典型工作任务的真实需求来设计,具有很强的实用性。

  三是互动性。本书每个模块都包括学习目标、任务情景、引导问题、理论介绍、经典范文、结构分析、写作指导、常用句型、问题解答、写作实训等部分,不同部分层层递进,要求师生、生生之间积极互动,完成相应的任务。

  四是立体化。本书作为教育部职业教育商务英语专业国家级教学资源库商务英语写作课程资源(网址:gczyk.36ve.com)以及广东省教育厅《商务英语写作》精品资源在线开放课程(网址:https://mooc.icve.com.cn/cms/)配套教材,配有视频微课、电子讲义、教学PPT等资源,方便广大师生进行线上线下混合式学习。

  本书既可以作为商务英语、应用英语、旅游英语、国际贸易、国际商务、涉外文秘等专业的教材,也可以作为教师、学生、相关从业人员手头必备的参考资料,还可以满足社会人士自学或考级需要。

  本书在编写过程中,参考了大量的相关资料,由于篇幅有限,未能一一列出,在此一并向这些资料的版权所有者表示感谢。由于客观原因,我们无法联系到您。如您能与我们取得联系,我们将在第一时间更正任何错误或疏漏。

  本书的编写得到了华南电商产业科技(深圳)有限公司朱加宝先生、广州联强信息技术有限公司张剑斌先生，以及相关兄弟院校教师的大力支持，在此一并表示衷心的感谢。

由于编者水平有限，书中难免存在疏漏与错误，恳请专家、学者、广大师生和外贸行家批评指正。各位读者可通过邮箱1309054070@qq.com与编者联系。

编者

2024年9月

目 录

Module 1	Writing for Job Hunting and Application	1
Task 1	Resume	1
Task 2	Cover Letter	13
Module 2	Writing for Daily Office Work	25
Task 1	Telephone Message	25
Task 2	Notice	33
Task 3	Memo	40
Task 4	Meeting Agenda	48
Task 5	Minutes	57
Module 3	Writing for Publicizing and Advertising	69
Task 1	Announcement	69
Task 2	Business Card	77
Task 3	Company Profile	85
Task 4	Product Introduction	96
Task 5	Recruitment Advertisement	105
Module 4	Writing for Business Etiquette	117
Task 1	Invitation Letter	117
Task 2	Acceptance Letter	127
Task 3	Refusal Letter	135
Task 4	Thank-you Letter	144
Task 5	Congratulation Letter	152
Task 6	Reservation Letter	161
Task 7	Complaint Letter	169
Task 8	Reply Letter to Complaint	177

Module 5　Writing for Business Report and Proposal······186
　　Task 1　Business Report ······186
　　Task 2　Business Proposal ······199

Appendix ······210

References ······217

Module 1 Writing for Job Hunting and Application

Task 1 Resume

 Learning Objectives

- Learn about the definition, function and types of resume.
- Be familiar with the structure, content and format of resume.
- Master the useful expressions such as words, phrases and sentences for resume.
- Be able to skillfully compose a correct resume in the real business situation.

 Task Situation

Mabel, a student from Foreign Language and Business College of Guangzhou Railway Polytechnic, majors in Business English and will graduate next June. Now, she is planning to look for a job as a business secretary.

Supposing you are Mabel, how do you prepare your resume?

 Questions

- What basic contents are included in a resume?
- How are the structure and format of a resume?
- What points should we pay attention to when composing a resume?

 Theory Background

Resume, also called Curriculum Vitae (CV) in Latin, is a brief written self-description about personal information, education background, work experience, qualifications, skills, etc.

It is one of the most essential documents used for further study or job hunting. Resume is mainly used to introduce the applicant himself or herself, draw the interviewer's attention or interest, and gain a personal interview opportunity.

According to the function and priority highlighted, resume can be classified into three types: chronological resume, functional resume and combination resume.

Sample Study

Sample 1: Chronological resume

Resume	
Name:	Chen Lili
Gender:	Female
Date of Birth:	May 2, 2002
Place of Birth:	Guangzhou, Guangdong
Marital Status:	Single
Health Condition:	Excellent
Address:	Guangzhou City Polytechnic
	No. 248, Guangyuan Middle Road, Baiyun District, Guangzhou
Phone:	139 ×××× ××××
E-mail:	lilichen@126.com
Wechat:	lilichen

Job Objective: To obtain a sales position in a foreign trade company

Education Background
Sep. 2020-Jul. 2023:   Guangzhou City Polytechnic
Sep. 2017-Jul. 2020:   Guangzhou No.6 Middle School

Work Experience
Summer 2022:   Manager assistant, Guangzhou Golden Foreign Trade Co. Ltd.
Summer 2021:   Salesgirl, Guangzhou Peak Sports Clothes Company

Qualifications and Skills
TEM-4, BEC-Higher, NCRE-2

Awards
Jun. 2022:   The First-class Prize of National Spoken English Contest
Mar. 2021:   School Merit Student

Hobbies
Traveling, drawing, reading

Personalities
Helpful, warm, outgoing

References
Available upon request

Sample 2: Functional resume

Resume

Liu Xiaoming
Job Objective: PR Manager in International Firm
Address: No. 7019, Yitian Road, Futian District, Shenzhen, Guangdong Province, China
Tel: 0755-××××　××××
E-mail: xmliu@hotmail.com

Qualification Summary
　　Professional and experienced in a fast-paced environment which demands for strong organizational, technical and interpersonal skills.
　　Trustworthy, ethical, and discreet, committed to superior customer service.
　　Confident and poised in interactions with individuals at all levels.
　　Detail-oriented and resourceful in completing projects.

Experience Highlights
1. Administrative Support
　　· Performed administrative and secretarial support functions for the President of a large sportswear manufacturer. Coordinated and managed multiple priorities and projects.
　　· Provided discreet secretarial and reception services for a busy family counseling center. Scheduled appointments, and maintained accurate and up-to-date confidential client files.
　　· Assisted with general accounting functions. Provided telephone support, investigated and resolved billing problems for an 18-member manufacturer's buying group. Trained and supervised part-time staff and interns.
2. Customer Service and Reception
　　· Registered incoming patients in a hospital emergency room. Demonstrated ability to maintain composure and work efficiently in a fast-paced environment while preserving strict confidentiality.
　　· Conducted patient interviews to elicit necessary information for registration, accurate prioritization, and to assist medical professionals in the triage process.

· Orchestrated hotel special events and reservations. Managed customer relations and provided exemplary service to all customers.

3. Management and Supervision

· Promoted rapidly from front desk clerk to assistant front office manager at an upscale hotel. Oversaw all operations including restaurant, housekeeping, and maintenance.

· Troubleshot and resolved problems, mediated staff disputes, and handled customer complaints.

· Participated in staff recruitment, hiring, training and scheduling. Supervised a front-desk staff.

Education and Training

· Management School of Cambridge University, MA (2012)
· Management School of Liverpool University, BA (2009)
· Public Relations Senior Training, Tsinghua University, 2018
· Higher Business Administrative Affairs, Peking University, 2016

Sample 3: Combination resume

Resume

Mark Peng

Job Objective: Supply chain manager or analyst for a manufacturing company

Address: No. 356, Dongfeng Middle Road, Yuexiu District, Guangzhou, Guangdong Province, China

Tel: 139 ×××× ××××

E-mail: markpeng@sina.com

Summary Qualifications

· Recent experience in manufacturing inventory, logistics and distribution. Three years' experience in data analysis, and over six years of diverse business management experience.

· Highly organized. Analytical thinker with strong communication skills.
· Exceptional liaison with global experience.
· Ambitious and flexible team member who loves to learn.
· Computer savvy.

Professional Experience

2016-Now, Guangzhou Baiyunshan Pharmaceutical Company

1. Data Analyzing & Coordinating

· Forecast and ordered production and shipment of over 20 million units per month, and analyzed sales data to accurately meet demand and emergency orders.

• Maximized manufacturing and distribution efficiency for up to 50 specialized product lines for two overseas plants, a U.S.-based distribution center, and four contract manufacturers.

• Received regular, outstanding feedback from managers and line staff in every plant.

2. Planning

• Juggled manufacturing schedules and equipment to achieve complex technical requirements such as narrow turnaround times, capacities, and temperature ranges.

• Ordered, tracked, and monitored inventory of supplies and finished goods system-wide, ensuring freshness and proper handling of critical substances, and accuracy in billing and record keeping.

• Prepared and analyzed statistical and productivity reports, and coordinated information management between two data-tracking applications.

3. Quality Monitoring

• Improved production processes and increased distribution center efficiency.

• Organized new product launches, and followed each product until it was available for sale, ensuring regulatory compliance and documentation.

• Identify and resolve quality assurance and other issues.

2013-2016, Ping'an Insurance Company

Demand Analyzing & Training Developing

• Identified client training needs by analyzing statistics; prepared winning proposals.

• Developed safety and loss control training materials for clients of an industrial insurance company.

• Developed and adapted quality PPT and written training materials to prepare employees to handle the full spectrum of industrial hazards.

 Sample Structure

1. Head/Title
2. Personal information
   2.1 Name
   2.2 Gender
   2.3 Date of birth
   2.4 Place of birth
   2.5 Marital status
   2.6 Health condition
   2.7 Address
   2.8 Telephone

> 3. Job objective
> 4. Education background
> 5. Work experience
> 6. Qualifications and skills
> 7. Awards
> 8. Hobbies
> 9. Personalities
> 10. References

 Structure Analysis

1. Head/Title: Located in the top middle; it usually writes as follows.

> Resume/ RESUME

2. Personal information: To state the applicant's name, address, telephone number, date of birth, marital status, health condition, etc.

Name:	Chen Lili
Gender:	Female
Date of Birth:	May 2, 2002
Place of Birth:	Guangzhou, Guangdong
Marital Status:	Single
Health Condition:	Excellent
Address:	Guangzhou City Polytechnic
	No. 248, Guangyuan Middle Road, Baiyun District, Guangzhou
Phone:	139 ×××× ××××
E-mail:	lilichen@126.com
Wechat:	lilichen

3. Job objective: To state the job position that the applicant is looking for.

> Job Objective: To obtain a sales position in a foreign trade company

4. Education background: To state the applicant's education experience, major, main courses studied, etc. in a reverse order.

Sep. 2020-Jul. 2023:   Guangzhou City Polytechnic
Sep. 2017-Jul. 2020:   Guangzhou No.6 Middle School

5. Work experience: To state the applicant's job position, work responsibility, achievement, etc. in a reverse order.

Summer 2022:   Manager assistant, Guangzhou Golden Foreign Trade Co. Ltd.
Summer 2021:   Salesgirl, Guangzhou Peak Sports Clothes Company

6. Qualifications and skills: To provide the recruiter with the qualifications and skills that the applicant has obtained.

TEM-4, BEC-Higher, NCRE-2

7. Awards: To present the prizes that the applicant has been awarded.

Jun. 2022:   The First-class Prize of National Spoken English Contest
Mar. 2021:   School Merit Student

8. Hobbies: To describe the things that the applicant likes doing best.

Traveling, drawing, reading

9. Personalities: To describe the applicant's character traits by using some adjectives.

Helpful, warm, outgoing

10. References: To provide some related certificates or documents as required.

Available upon request

 Writing Tips

1. Provide your full personal information such as name, telephone number, email, address, etc.
   2. Present your job objective with a verb phrase instead of a full sentence.
   3. List your education background with specialty, degree, main courses studied, etc.
   4. Describe your work experience with the position and responsibility you have undertaken.
   5. State your education background and work experience in a reverse order.
   6. Use dynamic verbs, vivid adjectives and active voice; do not use the subject "I".

7. Remember that a resume is used for obtaining a chance for an interview instead of a job.

8. Try to keep your resume not longer than one A4 page.

Useful Expressions

1. Job objective: To obtain a position in the human resources department of a multinational corporation.

求职目标：欲觅跨国公司人力资源部门一职。

2. To look for a challenging position related to computer design and application.

欲寻与电脑设计与运用相关的、具有挑战性的职位。

3. To apply for an entry-level salesperson position in a foreign trade company.

应聘外贸公司初级业务员职位。

4. Education background.

教育经历。

5. Graduate from Peking University.

毕业于北京大学。

6. Study at/in Guangzhou University.

在广州大学学习。

7. Major in marketing.

主修市场营销/专业为市场营销。

8. Receive a MA degree.

获文学硕士学位。

9. Excellent student leader.

优秀学生干部。

10. Secretary of Class League Branch.

班级团支部书记。

11. Work as a sales manager in a sino-foreign joint venture.

在中外合资企业担任销售经理。

12. Assist dealing with daily office affairs.

帮助处理日常办公事务。

13. In charge of new product promotion.

负责新产品推销。

14. Responsible for training employees and making sales plans.

负责培训员工，制订销售计划。

15. Handle unexpected incidents and customers' complaints.

处理突发事件和客户投诉。

16. Responsible for receiving and answering foreign trade partners' letters.

负责接收并回复国外贸易伙伴的信函。

17. References will be available upon request.

如有需要,可提供证明材料。

 Task Solving

After studying what has been presented above, you may know how to compose a resume successfully.

 Consolidation Exercise

1. Please fill in the blanks according to the initial letter.

Resume

Name: Mary

Gender: (1) F_____

Date of Birth: Dec. 1998

Place of Birth: Guangzhou, China

Marital Status: (2) S_____

Health: Good

Address: No. 58, Guangzhou Avenue, Baiyun District, Guangzhou, Guangdong, China

Phone: 156 ×××× ××××

Email: mary168@email.com

Wechat: mary168

Job (3) O_____:

Seek a position as a foreign trade (4) s_____ in a famous trade company

Education (5) B_____:

1. Sept. 2019-Jun. 2023: Jinan University, (6) m_____ in Business English with a focus on Business Secretary

2. Sept. 2016-Jun. 2019: Guangzhou No. 7 Middle School

Working (7) E_____:

1. Part-time salesgirl at Sunlight Company (2022)

2. Part-time service staff at McDonald's in Jianggao Town (2021)

3. Part-time receptionist at Dafang Cosmetics Co., Ltd (2020)

Qualifications and (8) S_____:

1. CET-6

2. Advanced Translation Certificate

3. NCRE-2

4. (9) P_____ in Microsoft Office

Awards:

1. "Top 10 Best Singers" at school

2. Second prize in a voice-over competition

Hobbies:

Traveling, singing, and reading

Personalities:

Enthusiastic, outgoing, and (10) e_____

2. Please translate the English underlined into Chinese.

Resume

Mandy Li

Guangdong University of Foreign Studies

No.2, Baiyun Avenue, Baiyun District, Guangzhou, Guangdong, China

(1) Job Objective: To seek for an English teaching position in a high school

Education Background

• (2) MA, College of English Education, Guangdong University of Foreign Studies, 2019-2022

• BA, College of Foreign Languages, Guangzhou University, 2015-2019

Work Experience

• Taught IELTS in Guangzhou Sunshine English Training School, part time, 2021

• (3) Taught oral English for English majors, Guangzhou Vocational University of Science and Technology, part time, 2020

• Worked as a translator at the 15th South China Economic Forum, 2018

Qualifications and skills

• TEM-8, 2019

• English Translation Certificate (III), 2018

Awards

• (4) Excellent graduate, 2022

• (5) The first prize of National Spoken English Contest, 2018

• The first-class scholarship, Guangzhou University, 2017

3. Please translate the Chinese in the brackets into English.

Resume

Name: Huang Fang

Date of Birth: May 16, 2002

Gender: Male

_____(婚姻状况): Single

Address: No. 261, Fuxing Road, Haidian District, Beijing

_____(求职目标): Seek a job as a computer programmer

Education:

Sep. 2020-Jul. 2022: Computer College of Peking University

Sep. 2017-Jul. 2020: Beijing No.4 Middle School

Language skills:

- _____(英语口语流利)
- CET-6
- BEC-II

_____(资格与技能)

- NCRE-1
- Certificate for Business Secretary

Hobbies:

Swimming, travelling, playing the guitar

Reference:

_____(如有需要可提供)

Writing Practice

Directions: Li Chen is a student from Computer College of South China University of Technology. He majors in software engineering. He wants to get a position for software programmer in a computer company. Supposing you are Li Chen, please write a resume according to the following Chinese hints.

简　历

姓名:李晨

性别:男

出生日期:2002年9月5日

婚姻状况:未婚

健康状况:良好

联系地址:广东省广州市天河区五山路381号

联系电话:020-××××　××××

求职目标:软件工程师

学习经历：

2018.09—2022.07:华南理工大学计算机学院

2015.09—2018.07:广州市第三中学

工作经历：

2022年至今:广州卡尔文计算机公司,助理工程师

所获荣誉：

2021年全国高校计算机能力挑战赛一等奖

2022年省级优秀毕业生

资格证书：

大学英语四级证书

计算机技术与软件专业技术资格(初级)

兴趣爱好：

旅游、阅读、集邮

佐证材料：

如有需要可提供

Module 1 Writing for Job Hunting and Application

Task 2 Cover Letter

 Learning Objectives

- Learn about the definition, function and types of cover letter.
- Be familiar with the structure, content and format of cover letter.
- Master the useful expressions such as words, phrases and sentences for cover letter.
- Be able to skillfully compose a correct cover letter in the real business situation.

 Task Situation

Mabel, a student from Foreign Language and Business College of Guangzhou Railway Polytechnic, majors in Business English and will graduate next June. Now, she is planning to look for a job. Yesterday (March 12, Monday) she read a recruitment advertisement (seen below) published on www.chinahr.com. It arises her interest and she is going to apply for it.

Vacancy for Secretary

Guangzhou Fortune Trade Company is looking for a business secretary now.

References:
1. Receive and answer phone calls, and take telephone messages
2. Greet visitors or customers and direct them to appropriate person
3. Schedule appointments, meetings and travels for general manager
4. Responsible for the daily meeting organizing and arrangement
5. Deal with paperwork such as writing notices, taking minutes, etc.
6. Compile materials for general manager and file business documents
7. Handle some temporary emergency affairs of the company
8. Perform other tasks related to the position of secretary

Requirements:
1. Guangzhou citizen, aged between 20 and 28 years old
2. With a college diploma or above, bachelor degree preferred
3. Major in secretary, Chinese, business English, etc.
4. With work experience or/and male preferable
5. Proficiency in spoken and written English, CET-6 preferable
6. Familiar with the use of Microsoft Office
7. Flexible mind and excellent service attitude

> 8. Warm, outgoing, diligent, responsible and honest
>
> Those who are interested in it, please kindly send your resume and a recent digital photo to gzft@126.com.
>
> Add: No.196, Tianhe North Road, Guangzhou, China
>
> Tel: 020-×××× ××××
>
> Fax: 020-×××× ××××
>
> Website: www.gzft.com
>
> E-mail: gzft@126.com
>
> Contact: Mr. Alexander, HR Manager

Supposing you are Mabel, how do you prepare your cover letter?

Questions

- What basic contents are included in a cover letter?
- How are the structure and format of a cover letter?
- What points should we pay attention to when composing a cover letter?

Theory Background

Cover letter, also called application letter, is a short and introductory letter written by a job seeker for getting an interview opportunity. It is a personal letter to the public.

It is one of the most important documents used for job hunting. Cover letter mainly serves to introduce the applicant himself or herself, draw the interviewer's attention or interest, and gain a personal interview opportunity.

According to the applicant with work experience or not, it can be classified into two types: cover letter written by one without work experience, and cover letter written by one with work experience.

Sample Study

Sample 1: Cover letter written by one without work experience

> Guangzhou City Polytechnic
>
> No.248, Guangyuan Middle Road
>
> Baiyun District, Guangzhou, China

Dear Mr. Henry,

    I am Chen Li. I read the position of secretary advertised by your company in *China Daily* yesterday. I am very interested in the position, so I am writing to apply for it.

    I major in business secretary and will be graduating from Guangzhou City Polytechnic next month. I have studied business management, document writing, business etiquette, secretary English and so on. I am one of the best students. My GPA has been in the top three of the grade for five consecutive terms.

    I have some practical experiences. I have interned in a foreign trade company, working as a business assistant in summer holidays. I was responsible for receiving customers, arranging travel itinerary and translating business documents, from which I have learned how to communicate and cooperate with others.

    I am very familiar with the use of Microsoft Office. I know how to skillfully use Word to edit documents and Excel to analyze data. Besides, I am proficient in English. I have passed CET-6 with a high score of 680, and I can fluently communicate with foreigners in English.

    I have been awarded the first-rate national scholarship twice. And I have won the special prize in the Hope Cup English Contest and the first prize in the National Trade Skills Competition.

    In a word, I believe that I am quite well qualified for the position of secretary in your company.

    Enclosed are my resume and one recent digital photo with this letter. I would be very grateful if you could give me an opportunity for a personal interview. I am looking forward to your early reply.

Truly yours,
Chen Li

Enclosures:
1. One resume
2. One recent digital photo

Sample 2: Cover letter written by one without work experience

July 1

Dear Sir or Madam,

    I am writing to express my strong interest in the open position at your company—Junior Business Development Representative published on your company's website.

    I am specializing in marketing and I will be graduating from Guangzhou University next month. I have studied core courses such as sales management, marketing planning, and business negotiation, which have given me a unique perspective on the marketing world. I am particularly proud of my senior thesis, which focused on consumer behavior and received an "A" grade.

During my university years, I have actively sought opportunities to improve myself so that I can better meet the demands of future job position. For example, through participation in relevant extracurricular activities, I have developed strong organizational and leadership skills. While serving as a part-time salesperson in Sunny Fitness Equipment Trade Company, I have gained some practical experiences related to the position. Besides, I have gained a smart new marketing qualification certificate.

I am excited about the opportunity to bring my enthusiasm and hard work to your team. As a self-motivated individual, I am not afraid of hard work and I am always looking for ways to improve myself. I believe that my strong communication skills and attention to details would enable me to make an immediate contribution to your organization.

I would be very appreciated if I am honored to get a chance for an interview. I am waiting for your early answer with keen desire.

Sincerely yours,

Mr. Wang

Sample 3: Cover letter written by one with work experience

March 22

Dear Mr. Peter,

I'm extremely interested in the technical director position posted by your company on https://www.liepin.com/, so I am writing to apply for it.

My enclosed resume reflects both my rich work experience and my MBA from Business School of Harvard University. The following highlights my qualifications.

*Worked as a core member of the technical team, building up the search advertising platform of Google and being mainly responsible for platform search engine optimization.

*Directed several key technical projects at Baidu, making detailed implementation plans to accomplish goals and directing the integration of technical activities.

*Served as Russia Chief at Alibaba, where I was responsible for analyzing and designing KPI analytical reports for the Alibaba Connect Application.

*Authored several technical white papers on social media advertising networks as a MBA student at Harvard University; asked to be a featured speaker at Internet Marketing Summit.

I am confident that my background provides the experience you required for this position. I look forward to the opportunity to discuss in details how my skills would benefit Tencent in achieving its goals. Thank you for your consideration and forthcoming response.

Yours faithfully,

David Song

Sample 4: Cover letter written by one with work experience

June 11

Dear Mr. Norman,

 I am applying for the position of financial manager that your company advertised in Washington Post on March 9.

 My varied work experience in financial and accounting services, coupled with my MA degree in accounting, has well prepared me for the position.

 I worked as an auditor in Red Star Accounting Firm, auditing and checking the original documents of various economic activities of customers. This work has given me a firsthand experience of auditing, and I have learned how to keep the company's financial activities legal and compliant.

 I also served as an accountant in New Hope Trade Company, and I am mainly responsible for conducting account processing, including filling in accounting vouchers, preparing statements, etc. which enables me make financial statement and analyze the financial situation of company.

 After you have reviewed my enclosed resume, I would appreciate having the opportunity to discuss with you why I believe I have the right qualifications to serve you and your clients. I can be reached by phone after 3:00 p.m. every day except weekends.

Sincerely,
Karl Green

Enclosure: resume

Sample Structure

1. Letterhead (if necessary)
2. Date
3. Salutation
4. Body (opening, middle, closing)
5. Complimentary close
6. Signature
7. Enclosure (if necessary)

Structure Analysis

 1. Letterhead: To show the writer's address, usually located in the left top corner.

> Guangzhou City Polytechnic
> No.248, Guangyuan Middle Road
> Baiyun District, Guangzhou, China

2. Date: To state when the letter is written, placed in the left top corner and just below the letterhead.

> May 10

3. Salutation: To show respect to the receiver, often laid in the top left corner and just below the inside address.

> Dear Mr. Henry
> Dear Sir or Madam
> To whom it may concern

4. Body: To state the main content that the letter is concerned about; it is the most important part and includes opening, middle and closing.

> I am Chen Li. I read the position of secretary advertised by your company in *China Daily* yesterday. I am very interested in the position, so I am writing to apply for it.
> ...
> Enclosed are my resume and one recent digital photo with this letter. I would be very grateful if you could give me an opportunity for a personal interview. I am looking forward to your early reply.

5. Complimentary close: To show the writer's courtesy, usually set in the bottom right corner and just above the signature.

> Truly yours
> Yours faithfully

6. Signature: To state by whom the letter is written; for the purpose of politeness, signature written in hand is preferred.

> Chen Li

7. Enclosure: To attach some documents or materials concerned but not convenient to state in the body part.

Enclosures:
1. One copy of resume
2. One recent digital photo

 ## Body Structure

The body usually consists of the following three parts.

1. Opening
2. Middle
3. Closing

 ## Body Analysis

1. Opening: To state the information source and express your interest as well as purpose for writing.

> I am Chen Li. I read the position of secretary advertised by your company in *China Daily* yesterday. I am very interested in the position, so I am writing to apply for it.

2. Middle: To briefly introduce yourself (educational background, work experience, qualifications, skills, etc.)

> I major in business secretary and will be graduating from Guangzhou City Polytechnic next month...
>
> I have some practical experiences. I have interned in a foreign trade company, working as a business assistant in summer holidays...
>
> I am very familiar with the use of Microsoft Office. I know how to skillfully use Word to edit documents and...
>
> I have been awarded the first-rate national scholarship twice. And I have won the special prize in the Hope Cup English Contest...

3. Closing: To express your thanks as well as your wishes or expectations.

> I would be very grateful if you could give me an opportunity for a personal interview. I am looking forward to your early reply.

Writing Tips

1. Target your letter at a specific person or position and get right to the point.
2. Highlight that you are the unique person for the position by showing your strengths.
3. Focus on what you can do for the company rather than why you need the job.
4. Make your letter appealing in content and correct in spelling, grammar and facts.
5. Check your spelling and ask someone else to proofread your letter before you send it.
6. Keep your letter within one page and each paragraph contains 3 or 4 sentences at most.

Useful Expressions

1. I have learned from a friend that there is a vacant position for marketing manager in your company.

我从朋友处获知贵公司有一个市场部经理职位空缺。

2. Your company advertised secretary position in *China Daily* yesterday. And my work experiences is just qualified for it.

贵公司昨天在《中国日报》上发布了秘书招聘广告,我的工作经历正好符合要求。

3. I am very interested in the manager assistant position your company published in *Guangzhou Morning Post* yesterday.

我对贵公司昨天刊登在《广州英文早报》上的经理助理职位非常感兴趣。

4. I would like to apply for the salesperson position posted on www.51job.com by your company.

我想申请贵公司发布在前程无忧网站上的销售员一职。

5. My name is Wang Fang, born in Guangzhou, and I am 23 years old.

我叫王芳,出生于广州,今年23岁。

6. I am Chen Lu, a Beijing native, 25 years old.

我叫陈路,北京本地人,今年25岁。

7. I specialized in financial technology during my university.

大学期间,我学的是金融科技专业。

8. I graduated from Peking University with a business administration major.

我毕业于北京大学工商管理专业。

9. I graduated from Cambridge University with a Bachelor's degree of arts last June.

我去年6月从剑桥大学毕业,获文学学士学位。

10. I completed my studies from Jinan University last September and received a Master's degree of engineering.

我去年6月从暨南大学毕业,获工程硕士学位。

11. I will be graduating from Guangzhou University with a Master's degree in Computer

Science this June.

我今年6月将从广州大学毕业，获计算机学硕士学位。

12.In addition to my excellent academic record, I also have rich practical experience.

我不但学业成绩优异，而且还有丰富的实践经验。

13.I have practiced working as a sales assistant in a foreign trade company in my spare time.

业余时间，我在一家外贸公司实习，担任销售助理。

14.During my university, I worked as an intern in a scientific and technical company. My job is developing applet.

大学期间，我在一家科技公司实习，工作内容是开发小程序。

15.After graduation, I have been serving as a chief accountant in a multinational corporation up to now.

从毕业至今，我一直在一家跨国公司担任总会计师。

16.From the attached resume, you can know that I have learned how to operate computers.

从所附简历，您可以了解到我已经学会了使用计算机。

17.I am good at using PS and PR software.

我擅长使用PS和PR软件。

18.I have a good command of English speaking and writing.

我有良好的英语口语和写作能力。

19.I am good at English listening, speaking, reading and writing.

我的英语听说读写都很优秀。

20.I am enclosing my detailed resume as well as one recent photo with this letter.

现随函附详细简历一份、近照一张。

21.Enclosed are my academic record and other references with this letter.

随函附成绩报告单及其他佐证材料。

22.Thank you for considering my application.

谢谢你考虑我的申请。

23.I will be very thankful for your consideration.

非常感谢你的考虑。

24.Your kind consideration will be greatly appreciated.

如能给予考虑，我将不胜感激。

25.I am looking forward to hearing from you soon.

期待早日收到您的回复。

Task Solving

After studying what has been presented above, you may know how to compose a cover letter successfully.

Consolidation Exercise

1. Please fill in the blanks according to the initial letter.

Dear Sir or Madam,

I am writing to express my (1) i_____ in the open position in your company. As an (2) e_____ and motivated individual with a strong background in marketing, I believe that I would be fit for this position.

In my previous position, I was (3) r_____ for managing the social media accounts of a large nonprofit organization. Through my (4) e_____, we were able to increase engagement and followers by over 20%. (5) A_____, I successfully created and implemented several marketing campaigns that increased brand awareness and donor revenue.

My (6) a_____ to work well under pressure and manage multiple projects simultaneously has (7) p_____ me for the challenges of this role. I am (8) c_____ that I can bring a fresh perspective and enthusiasm to your team, while also contributing to its overall success.

Thank you for (9) c_____ my application. I am eager to discuss my qualifications further and learn more about this opportunity. I look forward to the possibility of (10) j_____ your team and making meaningful contributions to its continued growth and success.

Sincerely yours,

Mary

2. Please translate the English underlined into Chinese.

Dear Hiring Manager,

(1) <u>I learned from your company's website that there is a vacant position for a sales manager.</u> I would like to apply for this position and showcase my abilities and experience.

My name is Smith Wang, and I have 10 years of sales experience. (2) <u>I have worked as a sales supervisor in a well-known company, managing a sales team</u> and successfully completing multiple important sales projects. (3) <u>I possess excellent communication skills and leadership abilities</u>, which allow me to establish strong relationships with clients and motivate team members to give their best performance.

Module 1 Writing for Job Hunting and Application

I have excellent sales knowledge and skills, including sales, negotiation skills, and market analysis abilities. I once worked for a multinational company and was responsible for developing the Chinese market. Through communication with clients, (4) I successfully developed a set of sales strategy suitable for the Chinese market and achieved good sales performance.

(5) I believe that my professional knowledge and experience can contribute to your company. If you need more information or an interview with me, please feel free to contact me.

Sincerely yours,
Smith Wang

3. Please translate the Chinese in the brackets into English.

April 18
Dear Mr. Wang,

　　I'm writing to _____ (应聘昨天贵公司网站上发布的销售一职). I am very interested in it.

　　I'm Lu Lin, 25 years old, and _____ (今年6月将从海南大学商学院毕业) with a Master's degree. My major is business administration. I have been among the best in our class in the past four years. I placed third in our college in the computer competition last year. _____ (在寒暑假期间,我获得了一些销售的实践经验) serving as a salesman in Xiuying Branch of Haikou Vanguard Supermarket. Besides, I am energetic, diligent, honest and responsible. _____ (我将为贵公司的进步和繁荣尽心尽力), if I have the honor to be employed by your company.

　　I have enclosed my resume, a recent photograph and a copy of my diploma as requested. I will be highly appreciated _____ (如能获得面谈的机会). I am looking forward to your early reply.

Sincerely yours,
Lu Lin

Writing Practice

Directions: Chen Lu learned that Shenzhen Grace Garments Co., Ltd. is looking for a salesperson from the website www.yingjiesheng.com yesterday (April 11). He is interested in the position and intends to apply for it. Supposing you are Chen Lu, please write a cover letter according to the following hints. More information can be added if necessary.

陈路,深圳人,2002年出生,就读于深圳职业技术大学外国语学院,主修商务英语,将于明年6月毕业。曾在某外贸公司实习,担任销售助理,协助销售经理做市场调研、产品推广,同时担任口译。通过全国大学英语六级考试,有全国计算机等级考试(二级)证书和跨境电子商务师证书,英语口语流利,熟练使用计算机。获全国大学生英语翻译能力竞赛一等奖,全国高校商业精英挑战赛国际贸易竞赛二等奖,获"广东省优秀大学生"荣誉称号。对人友好,容易相处,做事认真负责,具有团队精神。

Module 2　Writing for Daily Office Work

Task 1　Telephone Message

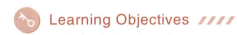 Learning Objectives

• Learn about the definition, function and types of telephone message.
• Be familiar with the structure, content and format of telephone message.
• Master the useful expressions such as words, phrases and sentences for telephone message.
• Be able to skillfully compose a correct telephone message in the real business situation.

 Task Situation

When Mabel is filing the meeting documents this morning, there is a phone call from Mr. Tony, the general manager of America Wilson Clothing Company. It is for Mr. Stephen, but he is out. So Mabel answers Mr. Tony. The dialogue between them is as follows.

> M=Mabel
> T=Tony
> M: Good morning. Guangzhou Fortune Trade Company. This is Mabel, secretary of general manager, speaking.
> T: Hello. May I speak to Mr. Stephen, the general manger of your company, please?
> M: I'm sorry. Mr. Stephen has just gone out. May I ask who is calling?
> T: This is Tony, the general manager of America Wilson Clothing Company. Do you know when he will be back?
> M: I really have no idea when Mr. Stephen would be back in the office. Could you call later or would you mind leaving a message?
> T: I think it's better for me to leave a message. But it's important and urgent. Please make sure he will get this message.
> M: I see. I'm sure to pass your message to Mr. Stephen.
> T: Good. Would you please tell him that due to some sudden changes we cannot ship the goods under S/C No. 266 within the prescribed time. I'll explain the reasons later.

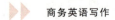

> M: Okay, let me repeat your message to see if I've got it all. And may I have your telephone number?
>
> T: My telephone is 433-××××and the area code is 648.
>
> M: Your telephone is 433-××××and the area code is 648. OK, I have got it. Goodbye.
>
> T: Thank you. Goodbye.
>
> Note:
>
> Date: June 6, Friday
>
> Time: 10:15

Supposing you are Mabel, how do you take a telephone message for Mr. Stephen?

 Questions

- What basic contents are included in a telephone message?
- How are the structure and format of a telephone message?
- What points should we pay attention to when composing a telephone message?

 Theory Background

Telephone message is a note written to keep an accurate record of incoming calls and left for the person who is off or absent.

Telephone message can help people who are away learn about the information of incoming calls, e.g. when the call is made, by whom the call is made, what the call is about and so on.

According to its content and function, telephone message can be classified into as many kinds as it can be.

 Sample Study

Sample 1

> **Telephone Message**
>
> Date: March 12
> Time: 11:45 a.m.
> From: Mr. Smith, Universal Electronics Company
> To: Mr. James
> Tel: 648-×××××××

26

Module 2 Writing for Daily Office Work

Message: He wants to know where and what time your next appointment with him will be. It is urgent and please call him back at an earlier time.

Written by: Janet

Sample 2

Telephone Message

To: Mr. Robert (Sales Department)
in your absence
From: Miss Cherry, Wisdom Trading Corporation
Tel: 9251-×××××××
leaving the following message

She has called twice saying that the alarm system we sold to her company did not work. Please phone her back as soon as possible.

Taken by: Morris

Sample 3

Telephone Message

Date: October 8   Time: 9:15 a.m.
From: Tom Jackson   To: Miss Mary
Tel: 0161-888-××××
(✔) Telephoned   (✔) Please ring back
(　) Call to see you   (　) Will call again
(　) Want to see you   (✔) Urgent
Message: Call to say your order will be delivered next Monday (June 25).

Message taker: Wendy

Sample 4

Telephone Message

Mr. Edwin,
    Miss Camille called to say that she would like to pay a business visit to our company with her delegation and discuss about the sales contract with you. If you are free, please ring her back at 604-777-××××.

Taker: Linda
Date: August 11
Time: 10:30 a.m.

 Sample Structure

1. Head/Title
2. Date and time
3. Message sender
4. Message receiver
5. Telephone number
6. Body
7. Message taker

 Structure Analysis

1. Head/Title: To state the subject matter of the message and it is usually written as follows.

Telephone Message; TELEPHONE MESSAGE

2. Date and time: To state the date and the time when the telephone message is taken.

Date: March 12
Time: 11:45 a.m.

3. Message sender: To state by whom the message is sent.

From: Mr. Smith, Universal Electronics Company

4. Message receiver: To state to whom the message is sent.

To: Mr. James

5. Telephone number: To state the message sender's telephone number so that he/she can be reached.

Tel: 648-×××　××××

6. Body: To state what the message is about. It should be written in indirect tone and clause.

Message: He wants to know where and what time your next appointment with him will be. It is urgent and please call him back at an earlier time.

7. Message taker: To state by whom the message is taken.

Written by: Janet

Writing Tips

1. Repeat the message to the caller to make certain you write down the right information.
2. Keep the message as short and concise as possible.
3. Make sure important information correct, complete and clear.
4. Highlight important information such as time, place, events concerned, etc.
5. Make the message easily understandable by listing the information items.
6. Transfer the message to the receiver as soon as it is completed.

Useful Expressions

1. Who is speaking?
您是哪位？

2. This is Bill speaking.
我是比尔。

3. May I speak to Mr. Li?
请问李先生在吗？

4. I'm sorry, but he is not in at the moment.
抱歉,他此刻不在这里。

5. Here is a telephone message from Mr. Park for you.
这是帕克先生给你的电话留言。

6. Please call back to confirm your booking for flight when you come back.
回来后请回电确认航班预订事宜。

7. He said he would ring later again.
他说他会再打电话过来。

8. Please ring him as soon as possible.
请尽快给他回电话。

9. Miss Lisa has just rung up saying that the goods you ordered have been packed as per request.
丽莎小姐刚刚来电话说你订购的货物已按要求包装好了。

10. A Mr. named Tom rung to ask when you were available.

有位叫汤姆的先生打电话来问你什么时候有空。

11. A man named Mr. Peter Wang has just rung up, saying that he will come to meet you next Tuesday.

一位叫王皮特的先生刚刚来电话说下周二会来见你。

12. Miss Harry called saying that she would be late for 20 minutes.

哈里小姐打电话来,说她可能要迟到20分钟。

13. Please call Mr. Hong at 8345 6788 about the order.

请打洪先生的电话8345 6788,问一下订单的事情。

14. Please tell him to call the general manager's office at 8642 3688.

请告诉他给总经理的办公室打电话,号码是8642 3688。

15. Mr. Smith called from Shanghai asking you to ring him back before 4:00 p.m. at any time tomorrow.

史密斯先生从上海打电话来,让你在明天下午4点前任何时候给他回电话。

16. You are requested to ring him up any time this evening from 8:00 to 10:00.

他让你晚上8点到10点之间给他打电话。

 Task Solving

After studying what has been presented above, you may know how to compose a telephone message successfully.

 Consolidation Exercise

1. Please fill in the blanks according to the initial letter.

Telephone Message

To: General Manager Mark
Date: January 4
Time: 10:00 a.m.

Message:
　　I (1) r_____ a call today from Mr. Smith, the President of Shanghai Silk Trade Company. He has (2) r_____ an urgent shipment before the (3) e_____ date of the letter of credit. It seems there is a high priority on fulfilling this order promptly (4) d_____ to their business needs.
　　The president emphasized the (5) i_____ of adhering to the deadline and expressed a (6) d_____ for us to (7) e_____ the timely dispatch of goods to maintain the strong business (8) r_____ between our companies.

If you wish to speak (9) d_____ with the president or someone else from Shanghai Silk Trade Company, I can arrange for a call at your earliest (10) c_____.

Message taken by: Mary

2. Please translate the English underlined into Chinese.

Telephone Message

Date: September 30th
Time: 10:30 a.m.

From: Mr. Bill, General Manager of Guangzhou Warner Ltd.
To: Sales Director of Guangzhou Sophia Foreign Trade Co., Ltd.
Tel: 020-×××× ××××

Message: Mr. Bill, (1) General Manager of Guangzhou Warner Ltd., was calling regarding (2) a delay in the delivery of the Ritz smartphones ordered by France Flanders Import-Export Co. Ltd. He just would like to inquire about (3) the current status of delivery and the expected time of arrival. If possible, (4) give him further information at your convenience during the day this week. He would like to suggest an alternative solution that would (5) help us to deliver the goods before the delivery deadline.

Message taker: Miss Cathy

3. Please translate the Chinese in the brackets into English.

Telephone Message

Date: December 22
Time: 9:15 a.m.

Dear Black,

_____(一位叫菲利普的先生给你打电话) this morning, _____(但是你不在). He asked you to _____ _____(今天下午4:30去他办公室). If you are convinced, _____(你务必给他回电话) at 020-×××× ×××× any time _____ _____(今天上午10:30到11:30之间).

Taken by: Linda

Writing Practice

Directions: Mary, a secretary of ABC Company, is working at her office at 9:55 a.m. July 16. At this time, the phone is ringing. She picks up the phone and answers it. The call is from Mr. Black, and it is for Mr. Smith, the sales director of company. But Mr. Smith is out. So Mary makes a telephone message and leaves it on Mr. Smith's desk. The following is the dialogue between Mary and Mr. Black. Please compose a telephone message according to their dialogue.

M＝Mary

B＝Mr. Black

M: Good morning. ABC Company.

B: Good morning. Could I speak to Mr. Smith, the sales director of your company, please?

M: I'm sorry. He's not in now. Could I ask who is calling?

B: This is Mr. Black of Australia Milk Powder Company. When will he be back?

M: He'll come back at about five in the afternoon. Would you like to leave a message?

B: Yes. Please tell him I will be in Guangzhou next Monday (July 20) and I want to have a further discussion about cooperation.

M: Can you give me your telephone number?

B: It's 658-××××. The area code is 0161.

M: So that's 0161-658-××××, Mr. Black.

B: Right. Thank you.

M: You are welcome. Good-bye!

B: Good-bye!

Task 2　Notice

 Learning Objectives

- Learn about the definition, function and types of notice.
- Be familiar with the structure, content and format of notice.
- Master the useful expressions such as words, phrases and sentences for notice.
- Be able to skillfully compose a correct notice in the real business situation.

 Task Situation

Mabel has successfully applied for the job position and now she is in the probationary period. As soon as she arrives at the office this morning (June 2, Monday), General Manager, Mr. Stephen tells her that he would like to hold a meeting about product sales and he asks Mabel to compose a notice informing all staff of sales department to attend the meeting. The details of the notice are as follows.

Subject: Sales meeting
Time: 2:30 p.m., June 6, Friday
Place: Room 609, Floor 6
Participants: All staff of sales department
Issued by: General Manager's Office

Supposing you are Mabel, how do you finish the task assigned to you?

 Questions

- What basic contents are included in a notice?
- How are the structure and format of a notice?
- What points should we pay attention to when composing a notice?

 Theory Background

Notice is a kind of written or oral means of communication used for passing on information to the public.

Notice serves many purposes from informing a meeting, a lecture, a match, publicizing a personnel change, a new policy, to announcing a new branch establishment, an office removal, etc. The versatility of notice makes it one of the most practical writings in business world.

According to in which format it is presented, notice can be classified into three types: bulletin notice, letter notice and memo notice.

According to the media of information communication, notice can be classified into three types: written notice, oral notice and broadcasting notice.

Additionally, according to the people concerned, notice can be classified into two types: inner notice and outer notice.

Sample Study

Sample 1: Bulletin notice

Notice

A meeting to assign workload hosted by HR manager will be held in Room 803, Floor 8 at 9:30 a.m. on September 7 (Tuesday).

All staff are requested to be present on time.

Those who are unable to attend the meeting, please call at 139 ×××× ×××× or 020-×××× ××××.

The HR Manager's Office

Guangzhou New Star Trade Company

September 2

Sample 2: Letter notice

Notice

May 8

Dear Guests,

The hotel will be undergoing a major renovation of the lobby, commencing on May 11 till 26. There may be noise made by the construction, which we will endeavor to keep to a minimum. However, any noise work will be from 9:00 a.m. to 18:00 p.m. every day with the exception of Sundays.

Please accept our sincere apologies for any inconvenience caused. If you need any assistance, please contact lobby manager at 8666 5533.

Yours truly,

Shelly Lin

General Manager

The Blue Sky Hotel

Sample 3: Written notice

NOTICE OF SALES MEETING

All salespersons are required to attend the year-end sales meeting to be held in the Headquarters Office from 9:00 a.m. until 11:30 a.m. on February 2 (Wednesday).

Lunch will be provided. The agenda will be e-mailed to you by the end of this month.

If you are unable to attend, please call me at 136 ×××× ×××× not later than January 28 and I will be thankful to you for doing that.

Sales Manager's Office
Emily Clothing Co., Ltd.
January 25

Sample 4: Oral notice

Notice

Hello, everyone. May I have your attention, please? I have something important to tell you.

A business banquet will be held in Room 1608, Rose Hall of China Hotel at 6:30 p.m. on July 16 (Friday). All staff are required to take part in it on time.

That's all. Thank you for listening.

Sample 5: Broadcasting notice

Broadcasting Notice

Ladies and gentlemen,

Attention, please! This is the customer service center of Wall Mart Broadcasting. Now Mrs. Smith is looking for her daughter, Betty. She is 8 years old, 1.25 meters tall, with short brown hair and in a pink coat and blue jean trousers. If anyone sees her, please call the customer service center at 8766 9103. If Betty hears this news, please go up straight to Room 602, Floor 6. Your mother is worriedly waiting for you.

Thank you!

 Sample Structure

1. Head/Title
2. Body
3. Company/Organization
4. Date

Structure Analysis

1. Head/Title: To state the subject matter of notice and it usually writes as follows.

> Notice, NOTICE, Notice of Board Meeting, NOTICE OF BOARD MEETING

2. Body: To state the main content that the notice is concerned about, such as the activity, time, place and other information; it is the most important part.

> A meeting to assign workload hosted by HR manager will be held in Room 803, Floor 8 at 9:30 a.m. on September 7 (Tuesday).
> All staff are requested to be present on time.

3. Company/Organization: To show by which company, organization, institution the notice is issued.

> The HR Manager's Office
> Guangzhou New Star Company

4. Date: To state when the notice is issued.

> September 2

 Writing Tips

1. Use small words, simple sentences and short paragraphs, and try to keep the notice as short and concise as possible, in order to convey the information to the reader within a short time.

2. Make sure the important information correct, complete and highlighted such as the time, place, events, person concerned, etc.

3. Employ graphic devices to make the heading eye-catching by using capitals, boldface, or italics and the body easily understandable by using numbered points or asterisks to distinguish some information.

4. Make your notice sound personal by using singular expression in the salutation (i.e. "Dear Customer", NOT "Customers") and individual terms (i.e. "you", NOT "all of you") in the message.

5. Make sure the notice is correct in grammar, check your word spelling and ask someone else to proofread your notice before you publish it.

Useful Expressions

1. Please be informed that...
敬请周知:……

2. Please be aware of...
敬请注意:……

3. Attention, please!
大家请注意。

4. Please keep quiet!
请保持安静。

5. May I have your attention, please? I have something important to tell you...
大家请注意:我有一件重要的事情要通知……

6. A meeting to assign workload by the executive manager is to be held in Room 403, Floor 4 at 9:30 a.m., Tuesday, November 7.
由总经理主持的有关工作任务安排的会议将于11月7日(周二)上午9:30在4楼403室举行。

7. A lecture on "How to Improve Sales Strategies" will be held in the department conference room at 2:30 p.m. on Tuesday (May 12).
一场关于如何提高销售策略的讲座将于周二(5月12日)下午2:30在部门会议室举行。

8. It is hereby announced that upon the decision of the Board of Directors, Mr. Black is appointed Personnel Manager.
经董事会决定,任命布莱克先生为人事部经理,特予公告。

9. The meeting scheduled to be held this Tuesday afternoon is postponed until further notice.
原计划本周二下午召开的会议推迟,具体时间另行通知。

10. This evening party will be under the auspices of (hosted by)/sponsored by/jointly sponsored by China Mobile Communication Corp Tianhe Branch.
本次晚会将由中国移动天河营业厅主办/赞助/联合赞助。

11. All staff members are requested to participate in the sales meeting on time.
所有员工务必准时参加销售会议。

12. Everyone is required to be present at a given time.
所有人务必准时出席。

13. Your participation is welcome.
欢迎您参加。

14. Do be present on time.
请准时到场。

15. Don't be late.
请勿迟到。

16. If you are unable to attend the meeting, please call me at 020-××××　×××× not later than February 27.

如无法参加会议，请于2月27日前联系我，电话号码是020-××××　××××。

Task Solving

After studying what has been presented above, you may know how to compose a notice successfully.

Consolidation Exercise

1. Please fill in the blanks according to the initial letter.

Notice

Dear senior managers,

　　With the continuous (1) e_____ of our business and the fierce market competition, we (2) f_____ understand that enhancing the leadership abilities of our management team is (3) c_____ for the long-term development of our company. Therefore, we have decided to organize a (4) p_____ management training for senior managers, which will take place from March 21 to March 29, in our company's (5) c_____ room.

　　The training will cover the (6) l_____ management concepts, leadership enhancement, team building, decision analysis and other (7) a_____. We have invited well-known management (8) e_____ in the industry to serve as the main speakers for this training. By then you will have the opportunity to communicate face-to-face with them.

　　We kindly request that you (9) c_____ your participation by replying to me not later than March 18 and arrive at the training venue on time. (10) E_____ please find the relevant training documents for you.

Mary
Secretary of Maxim Company

---

2. Please translate the English underlined into Chinese.

Notice

September 11

　　(1) <u>The 136th Canton Fair will be held in October at the Pazhou Complex in Guangzhou, China.</u> This event is expected to attract thousands of overseas exhibitors, particularly those associated with the Belt and Road Initiative (BRI).

The Canton Fair is an important trade show (2) providing a platform for domestic and international businesses to showcase their products and services. As a leading international trade fair, (3) it shows a range of exhibits such as machinery, electronics, household goods, textiles, and clothing.

Exhibitors and attendees should be aware that hotel accommodations and transportation in Guangzhou may be challenging during the fair. (4) We recommend that you arrange your business itinerary in advance such as departure time, booking hotel to minimize time spent in commuting.

Please come prepared for a successful trade show experience at Canton Fair 2024. (5) We are eagerly looking forward to your visit and wish you a pleasant and unforgettable experience.

The Organizing Committee of the 136th Canton Fair

3. Please translate the Chinese in the brackets into English.

Notice

July 6

Heads of all departments,

_____(将要举办一场财务会议) at Room 904 of Office Building at 2:00 p.m. on July 17 (Friday). _____
(届时将会讨论财务报告), so you had better prepare in advance. _____
_____(相关文件我会通过邮件发给大家).
_____(各位务必准时参会). Please call me at 020-×××× ×××× not later than July 11 _____(如不能参加会议).

The Administrative Office

Writing Practice

Directions: Mr. Nelson has been promoted to the finance director of company. Miss Black, the general manager, is going to hold an appointment meeting and announce it. She asks Chen Lu to compose a meeting notice for her. Supposing you are Chen Lu, please write a notice according to the following information.

Meeting subject: Appointment meeting
Meeting time: 9:30 a.m., March 10, Monday
Meeting place: Room 1608
Participants: All staff
Issued by: The General Manager's Office
The date: March 2

Task 3 Memo

Learning Objectives

- Learn about the definition, function and types of memo.
- Be familiar with the structure, content and format of memo.
- Master the useful expressions such as words, phrases and sentences for memo.
- Be able to skillfully compose a correct memo in the real business situation.

Task Situation

When Mabel arrived at office this morning (Tuesday, May 28), she found a note on her desk written by General Manager, Mr. Stephen. The details of the note are as follows.

> Write a memo under my name to all staff, telling all staff that a new entrance guard system has been installed in the office building and they should update their employee cards in the security department within this week. The memo is written on May 28.

Supposing you are Mabel, how do you finish the task assigned to you?

Questions

- What basic contents are included in a memo?
- How are the structure and format of a memo?
- What points should we pay attention to when composing a memo?

Theory Background

Memo is short for the Latin word memorandum. It means "things to be remembered". Memo, as a business document, is a way of written communication frequently used within a company.

Memo can be used to communicate information, announce decision, give instructions, make requests, offer suggestions, ask for information, explain reasons and so on. As far as formality is concerned, a memo is something between a business letter and a note. The language can be made more relaxed than in business letters. However, there is no excuse for the sentences to be chatty or impolite.

According to its content and function, memo can be classified into five types: meeting memo, instruction memo, notification memo, suggestion memo and reminder memo.

 Sample Study

Sample 1: Memo for training

Memo

To: All staff of administrative department
From: Philip, Executive Manager
Subject: Secretarial Training Schedule
Date: April 24

Dear all staff,

　　We are going to arrange a series of secretarial training courses next month. The courses are as follows:

　　(1) Typewriting;

　　(2) Secretary English;

　　(3) Business writing;

　　(4) Office equipment operation;

　　(5) Office management.

　　Please note that these courses will be free of charge to all administrative staff on the basis of the first-come-first-served.

　　Enclosing the course schedule and the registration method.

Enclosures:

(1) The course schedule;

(2) The registration method.

Sample 2: Memo for complaint

Memo

To: Ma Ming
From: Cathy
Subject: Mr. Li's complaint
Date: May 18

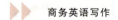

Dear Mr. Ma,

Thanks for your call this morning to discuss Mr. Li's complaints about his stay in our hotel. From the survey result, it seems obvious that our hotel service is far from satisfactory.

I attach my reply to Mr. Li from which you will see I have promised him one week's free accommodation for two at our hotel. I ask him to contact you soon at a suitable date.

When you visit Paris next week, please give this matter top priority. And you are required to prepare a detailed recommendation for immediate improvement. Our next regional meeting is on May 28, so I hope to read your report by May 26 and we will discuss it during the meeting.

Thanks for your help.

Cathy

Sample 3: Memo for meeting

Memo

To: All Sales Staff
From: Wang Nan, Sales Manager
Subject: Quarterly Meeting
Date: January 12

Dear All,

We will have a general meeting on September 29. The meeting will focus on our counter-measures in sales in the light of the current global economic crisis and high inflation. In addition to your general monthly report in PowerPoint, your suggestions are also more than welcome.

In case you are absent, please ask for leave well in advance and send your application for leave to our office secretary, Miss Joe. She will later show you the minutes of the meeting to keep you well informed.

Look forward to seeing you there.

Enclosures: Meeting agenda

Sample Structure

1. Head/Title
2. Memo receiver

> 3. Memo sender
> 4. Subject
> 5. Date
> 6. Body
> 7. Enclosure (if necessary)

 Structure Analysis

1. Head/Title: To state the subject matter of memo and it usually writes as follows.

> Memo, MEMO, Memo for Meeting, MEMO FOR MEETING

2. Memo receiver: To state whom the message is sent to.

> To: All staff of administrative department

3. Memo sender: To state by whom the message is sent.

> From: Philip, Executive Manager

4. Subject: To state what the memo is about.

> Subject: Secretarial Training Schedule

5. Date: To state when the memo is written.

> Date: April 24

6. Body: To state the main content that the memo is concerned about; it is the most important part.

> We are going to arrange a series of secretarial training courses next month. The courses are as follows:
> ...
> Please note that these courses will be free of charge to all administrative staff on the basis of the first-come-first-served.

7. Enclosure: To attach some documents or materials concerned but not convenient to state in the body part.

> Enclosures:
> (1)The course schedule;
> (2)The registration method.

Writing Tips

1. Simple words are always the first choice for memo, and short sentences and paragraphs are also preferred.

2. Make your memo concise, clear and to-the-point, and remember one memo for one matter or topic.

3. The tone used should be appropriate for the subject, audience and purpose; the active voice are preferred.

4. Keep your memo focusing on a single topic and thus make the reader concentrate on the subject.

5. Make your writing sound polite and thoughtful, and convey your sincere attitude towards your readers.

6. Use typographical devices such as asterisks, underlining, bold or italics to highlight important information.

7. Make your memo easy for your readers to understand by using headings, section headings, bullets or lists.

8. Revise, proofread and edit your memo before you send it out; otherwise any mistake might cause negative effects.

Useful Expressions

1. Thanks for your call this morning to discuss with me about Mr. Li's complaints to our hotel.
谢谢你今天早上来电和我讨论李先生对我们酒店的投诉问题。

2. Below/Here is the financial meeting (conference) arrangement (schedule).
以下是财务会议的安排。

3. The following is the latest status for our product sales.
以下是我们产品销售的最新状况。

4. Please take note that the latest products have arrived.
请注意最新产品已经到了。

5. Please remember to give this matter top priority when you are going to Paris next week.
请记住,当你下周到巴黎的时候,把此事列为头等重要事项。

6. This measure is on trial and you are welcome to put forward some suggestions on how it may work.
这项措施在试行中,欢迎对措施如何运行提出建议。

7. Please help follow up the sales plans made at last meeting.
请帮忙跟进上次会议制订的销售计划。

8. I would like to get necessary references before May 15.

我希望在5月15日前得到相关参考资料。

9. Please ensure production safety.

请确保生产安全。

10. You are required to prepare a detailed recommendation for immediate improvement.

你务必准备好一份详细的即刻改进的建议书。

11. I would like to get your report by February 26 so that we can discuss it at next meeting.

我希望在2月26日前收到你的报告,以便我们在下次会议上讨论。

12. I would be highly appreciated if you could send me your report before Thursday.

若能在周四前把你们的报告给我,我将十分感激。

13. Attached/ Enclosed are the meeting minutes.

附上会议记录。

14. Attaching/ Enclosing some proposals.

附上一些提议。

 Task Solving

After studying what has been presented above, you may know how to compose a memo successfully.

 Consolidation Exercise

1. Please fill in the blanks according to the initial letter.

Memo

To: Executive Manager David
Date: December 31
Time: 2:30 p.m.
Subject: Year-end Ceremony

The year-end ceremony is (1) s_____ at 2:30 p.m. on December 31 in the (2) b_____ hall of Guangzhou Rose Hotel. This ceremony (3) a_____ to recognize (4) o_____ employees and celebrate our (5) a_____ of the past year.

To ensure this event run (6) s_____, we have made careful (7) a_____ for venue decoration, catering, and program performances. (8) P_____ will be awarded to our deserving employees.

(9) F_____ or suggestions are welcome. Please call me at 020-××××××× before December 26 if you can not (10) a_____ the ceremony. Many thanks for your cooperation.

2. Please translate the English underlined into Chinese.

Memo

To: All employees
From: HR department
Subject: Purchase of fall work uniforms
Date: End of August

This is to inform you that the company has decided to (1) <u>purchase new work uniforms for all employees</u>. The new uniforms are expected to be delivered before the end of September.

In order to (2) <u>ensure that the new uniforms fit perfectly</u>, we request that all employees, including management personnel, (3) <u>provide your clothing sizes to the HR department</u> before the end of August.

Please send your size requests to hr.merits@yahoo.com or (4) <u>bring them to the HR department in person</u>.

(5) <u>Thanks for your cooperation on this matter</u>. We look forward to receiving your size requests soon.

3. Please translate the Chinese in the brackets into English.

Memo

To: GTS Staff
From: General Manager of GTS
Subject: Commendation—TRC Project
Date: April 18

The purpose of this memo is _____(正式嘉奖全体销售人员) for their _____（重大和突出的贡献）to the TRC Project. Their enthusiasm, sales strategy and product knowledge were pivotal to _____ _____（及时成功地完成该计划）.

_____（感谢他们出色的工作）and dedication, the company will _____（发放5000元奖金）to each of the member of the sales department next week.

Please let me know if you have any questions or advice.

Writing Practice

Directions: Supposing you are Mary, working as the secretary of Mr. David, HR manager in Guangzhou Karl's Clothing Company. Mr. David asks you to write a memo to all staff of sales department, informing them that the notebooks printed with our company's logo, name and address, which are to be given to customers, have arrived and will be available to them next Wednesday (December 12). You need to know the number of notebooks each member of sales department requires not later than December 10. The memo is written on December 2.

Task 4　Meeting Agenda

Learning Objectives

- Learn about the definition, function and types of meeting agenda.
- Be familiar with the structure, content and format of meeting agenda.
- Master the useful expressions such as words, phrases and sentences for meeting agenda.
- Be able to skillfully compose a correct meeting agenda in the real business situation.

Task Situation

Recently there have been some problems about product sales. In order to solve these problems, Mr. Stephen is going to hold a sales meeting at Room 609, Floor 6 at 2:30 p.m. (June 6, Friday). Therefore he asks Mabel to compose an agenda according to the following information.

> Mr. Stephen will host the meeting and read the minutes of last meeting (May 27).
> Lucy, sales manager, will report the problems about product sales.
> All department staff are required to present some suggestions for the problems.
> Mr. Stephen will conclude the meeting.
> Mr. Stephen will declare the time, date and place of next meeting and the adjournment of this meeting.

Supposing you are Mabel, how do you finish the task assigned to you?

Questions

- What basic contents are included in a meeting agenda?
- How are the structure and format of a meeting agenda?
- What points should we pay attention to when composing a meeting agenda?

Theory Background

Meeting agenda is a list of items or topics to be discussed, decided or declared during a specific meeting in a certain order. It is usually circulated or distributed among the participants before the meeting starts. Meeting agenda is very useful and has different functions.

Firstly, it communicates important information such as the meeting subject, time, date, place, host, the topics for discussion, the time allotment for each topic, and the speaker for each topic, etc.

Secondly, it provides attendees with what will be discussed or decided during the meeting so that they can make good preparations in advance.

Thirdly, it makes sure the meeting can focus on topics and run smoothly thus saving time and enhancing efficiency.

According to its content and function, meeting agenda can be classified into as many kinds as it can be.

 Sample Study

Sample 1: Agenda of board meeting

Agenda of Board Meeting

Date: December 14, Monday
Time: 2:30 p.m.
Place: Room 508, Floor 5

Attendees: Mr. Smith, Executive Director
          Mr. David, Personnel Director
          Mr. Mark, Financial Director
          Mr. William, Sales Director
Chairperson: Mr. Henry, General Manager

Items:
1. Call to order by chairperson Mr. Henry, General Manager
2. Read the minutes of last meeting by Mr. Smith, Executive Director
3. Issues for discussion
(1) Staff training plan put forward by Mr. David, Personnel Director
(2) Annual budget report proposed by Mr. Mark, Financial Director
(3) Marketing program presented by Mr. William, Sales Director
4. Any other business (AOB)
5. Time, date and place of next meeting
6. Adjournment

Sample 2: Agenda of project team meeting

Agenda of Project Team Meeting

Date: August 10, Friday
Time: 09:00 a.m.
Place: Room 1206
Attendees: Andrew, Sandy, Hunter, Julie, Steven
Chairperson: Mr. Philip, Executive Director
Issues:
1. 09:15   Approve of the minutes of last meeting by vote (Mr. Philip)
2. 09:30   Report on Canada investment project (Sandy)
3. 09:50   Discuss Canada investment project (All)
4. 10:00   Present the design concept of new products (Hunter)
5. 10:30   Explain the changes of export procedures (Julie)
6. 11:00   Discuss the challenge from rivals at home and abroad (All)
7. 11:30   Any other business
8. 12:00   Information of next meeting (Steven)
9. 12:05   Adjournment (Mr. Philip)

Sample 3: Agenda of executive committee meeting

Agenda of Executive Committee Meeting

Date: April 6, Wednesday
Time: 14:00 p.m.
Place: Council chamber
Attendees: Samuel, Elizabeth, Chris, Mark, Brown, Chelsea, Laura, Vincent
Absentees: Janet, Samuel
Chairperson: Mr. Andrew, Executive Director
Agenda:
1. Executive Director Mr. Andrew declares the meeting open
2. Secretary Elizabeth calls the roll and reports absentees
3. All approve of the minutes of last meeting by vote
4. General Manager Chris reviews on Tokyo project
5. Financial Director Mark reports the profit of last quarter
6. PR Manager Brown discusses other business
7. Secretary Elizabeth declares the details of next meeting
8. Executive Director Mr. Andrew adjourns this meeting

Sample Structure

1. Head/Title
2. Date, time and place
3. Attendees
4. Host/Chairperson
5. Items/Topics
6. AOB(any other business)
7. Information of next meeting
8. Adjournment

 Structure Analysis

1. Head/Title: To state the subject matter of a meeting agenda and it usually writes as follows.

Agenda, AGENDA, Agenda of Board Meeting

2. Date, time and place: To state the date, time and where the meeting will be held.

Date: December 14, Monday
Time: 2:30 p.m.
Place: Room 508, Floor 5

3. Attendees: To state the persons who will attend the meeting.

Attendees: Mr. Smith, Executive Director; Mr. David, Personnel Director; ...

4. Host/Chairperson: To state by whom the meeting will be hosted or chaired.

Chairperson: Mr. Henry, General Manager

5. Items/Topics: To list the main issues to be discussed, decided or declared at the meeting in order; it is the most important part.

Items:
1. Call to order by Chairperson Mr. Henry, General Manager
2. Read the minutes of last meeting by Mr. Smith, Executive Director
3. Issues for discussion:
...

6. AOB(any other business): To state other items or topics that will be discussed during the meeting.

Any other business (AOB):
…

7. Information of next meeting: To state what time, date and where the next meeting will be held.

Time, date and place of next meeting:
…

8. Adjournment: To state what time the meeting will be finished.

12:05	Adjournment

Writing Tips

1. Keep it concise and you only write down what is really related with the meeting subject.
2. List the procedures of meeting and outline the main points in a list such as 1, 2, 3, etc.
3. Make sure all important issues or topics are included in the agenda without any missing.
4. Make your agenda appealing in content and correct in spelling, grammar and facts.
5. Keep the body easily understandable by using numbered points, asterisks or checklists.
6. The tone and voice used in meeting agenda should be appropriate for the subject, audience and purpose.

Useful Expressions

1. Call to order by Chairperson Mr. Black.
主席布莱克先生会宣布会议正式开始。
2. Secretary Nancy calls the roll and reports absentees.
秘书南茜点名并报告缺勤情况。
3. Mr. David will host the meeting and read the minutes of last meeting.
大卫先生将主持会议并宣读上次会议的纪要。
4. The minutes of last meeting will be discussed and approved by vote.
讨论并表决通过上次会议的纪要。
5. The decision made during last meeting will be declared by Mr. Black.
布莱克先生宣布上次会议的决定。

6. Discussion will be continued on the unfinished topics of last meeting.

将继续讨论上一次会议未完成的议题。

7. The discussion of this meeting will focus on the following areas.

本次会议讨论的议题主要包括以下几个方面。

8. The subjects to be discussed during the meeting is about customer service.

会议期间要讨论的主题是客户服务问题。

9. Lucy, sales manager, will report the problems about product promotion.

销售经理露西将汇报产品促销问题。

10. Cathy, general manager, will put forward specific solutions to customers' complaints.

总经理凯西将就客户的投诉提出具体的解决方案。

11. Mr. Robinson will present the ways to deal with the negative effects brought by the counterfeit products in the market.

罗宾逊先生将汇报应对市场上假冒产品导致的负面影响的方法。

12. All department heads and the board will discuss the report presented by human resources director.

各部门领导和董事会将讨论人力资源总监提交的报告。

13. The last procedure is to vote on the motion of this meeting.

最后一个议程是对这次会议的提案进行表决。

14. Mr. White will conclude this meeting.

怀特先生将总结此次会议。

15. Mr. Smith will declare the time, date and place of next meeting and the adjournment of this meeting.

史密斯先生会宣布下次会议的时间、日期、地点以及休会。

Task Solving

After studying what has been presented above, you may know how to compose a meeting agenda successfully.

Consolidation Exercise

1. Please fill in the blanks according to the initial letter.

Agenda for Next Year's Strategic Goal Setting Meeting

Date: December 22, Monday
Time: 14:00 p.m.
Place: Room 1209

(1) A_____:
General Manager, Mr. Denny
Sales Manager, Mr. Brown
HR Manager, Mr. Philip
Financial Manager, Mr. Bill
(2) C_____: CEO, Mr. Edward

Items

1. Declare the meeting (3) o_____ (CEO, Mr. Edward)
2. Set the company's (4) s_____ goal for next year and assign task for each department (General Manager, Mr. Denny)
3. Analyze market (5) t_____, competitors and consumers' behavior, etc. (Sales Manager, Mr. Brown)
4. Develop staff (6) r_____ plan and decide staff training courses for the following year (HR Manager, Mr. Philip)
5. Analyze the company's financial situation and make (7) i_____ plan for the next year (Financial Manager, Mr. Bill)
6. (8) S_____ the discussion results and define the next action plan (General Manager, Mr. Denny)
7. Discuss any other (9) b_____ (All attendees)
8. Declare the details of next meeting and (10) a_____ this meeting (CEO, Mr. Edward)

2. Please translate the English underlined into Chinese.

Agenda of Promotion Meeting for
Introducing Advanced Production Equipment

Date: August 8 (Tuesday)
Time: 10:00 a.m.
Place: Room 606, Floor 6
Attendees:
Miss Alice (Marketing Manager)
Mr. Black (Production Manager)
Miss Carmela (Operations Manager)
Miss Dora (Secretary)
Chairperson: Mr. Smith (General Manager)

Agenda:

1. Mr. Smith will host the meeting at 10:00 a.m.

2. Mr. Smith will (1) <u>make a short opening remarks about the necessity of advanced production equipment</u>.

3. Miss Dora will read the minutes of last meeting (August 1).

4. Miss Alice will (2) <u>provide reference for the company's equipment procurement from marketing perspective</u> such as price, characteristics, etc.

5. Mr. Black will (3) <u>focus on the importance of new equipment in improving the company's production capacity</u> and enhancing market competitiveness on production levels.

6. Miss Carmela will (4) <u>give a detailed demonstration of the equipment's operation and its impact on operation level</u>.

7. Free Discussions related to the equipment.

8. Mr. Smith will (5) <u>make a summary about the key points of the discussion, wrap up the meeting</u> and declare the time, date and place of next meeting.

9. Adjournment by Miss Dora.

3. Please translate the Chinese in the brackets into English.

Agenda of Product Promotion Fair

Date: July 13, Monday

Time: 2:30 p.m.

Place: Room 908, Floor 9

Attendees: Mr. David, Miss Laura, Mr. Frost, Mr. Wood

Chairperson: Mr. David

Agenda:

1. General Manger Mr. David will _____ (正式宣布会议开始).

2. Secretary Miss Laura will _____ (宣读5月27日的会议记录).

3. Design Manager Mr. Frost will _____ (讲解产品促销会流程).

4. Marketing Manager Mr. Wood will _____ (陈述产品促销策略).

5. The procedures of questions and answers.

6. Any other business (AOB).

7. General Manger Mr. David will _____ (宣布下次会议的时间、日期、地点).

8. Adjournment

Writing Practice

Directions: Suppose you are Lucy, a secretary working in Fair-lady Clothing Company. Your general manager, Mr. Clark, would like to hold a quarterly meeting in Room 303, Floor 3 at 9:00 a.m. on July 6 (Tuesday). He asks you to make a meeting agenda according to the following main items to be discussed during the meeting.

> General Manager Mr. Clark will host the meeting and read the meeting minutes of June 27.
>
> Technology Manager Mr. Vincent will report the methods of improving the company's website.
>
> Customer Manager Mr. Black will present the strategies on how to deal with customers' complaints.
>
> HR Manager Miss Laura will explain the employees' training plan as well as incentive scheme.
>
> General Manager Mr. Clark will conclude this meeting, declare the time, date and place of next meeting and adjourn this meeting.

Module 2　Writing for Daily Office Work

Task 5　Minutes

 Learning Objectives

- Learn about the definition, function and types of minutes.
- Be familiar with the structure, content and format of minutes.
- Master the useful expressions such as words, phrases and sentences for minutes.
- Be able to skillfully compose correct minutes in the real business situation.

 Task Situation

Today (June 6, Friday) the sales meeting is being held in Room 609, Floor 6. It begins at 2:30 p.m. and ends at 5:00 p.m. Mr. Stephen hosts the meeting and Mabel is in charge of making minutes. Mike (Sales Manager), Frank, and Alice are present, but Peter is absent for apologies. The meeting is about the product sales problems.

> First, Mr. Stephen read the minutes of last meeting (May 31) and all participants approved it.
> Second, Mr. Mike, the sales manager, reported customers' feedback that iPhones were hard to find in the counters and iPads, the best-selling products for several months, didn't sell very well now. It's urgent to find out the reasons.
> Third, Mr. Frank said that the iPhones were available in the counters, but they were put on the bottom shelves. It was advised to display them on the top shelves.
> Fourth, Miss Alice said that we could increase the iPad sales volume by launching special promotions such as reducing the price, and sending free gifts.
> At last, Mr. Stephen concluded this meeting, declared that next meeting would be held in Room 609, Floor 6, at 2:30 p.m. on June 13 (Friday), and adjourned this meeting.

Supposing you are Mabel, how can you finish the assignment to you?

 Questions

- What basic contents are included in minutes?
- How are the structure and format of minutes?
- What points should we pay attention to when composing minutes?

57

Theory Background

Minutes are a written record of the proceedings of a meeting. Namely, minutes are often used to record the main topics or issues discussed, proposed, declared or decided during the meeting in order. Besides, minutes are also a reflection of the underlying meaning of the speaker's speech at the meeting. Therefore, the minutes-taker must understand not only what the speaker said but also what they really meant. Minutes are very important and can serve as the following functions: helping the attendees to recall what has been done at the meeting and prepare for the next meeting; providing the absentees with issues discussed, decisions reached, motions made and actions to take; serving as a well-kept file for further reference or inquiry.

According to their content and function, minutes can be classified into as many different kinds as they can be.

Sample Study

Sample 1: Minutes of all department heads

Minutes of All Department Heads
Date: July 17, Thursday
Time: 3:00 p.m.
Place: Room 403
Attendees:
Mr. Mark (HR Manager)
Mr. Peter (Marketing Manager)
Miss Kate (Production Manager)
Miss Janet (Secretary)
Absentee: Mr. Black
Chairperson: Mr. Hunter (General Manager)
1. Items
(1) Mr. Hunter read the minutes of last meeting (July 8) and all approved it.
(2) Mr. Mark reported the overtime issue, and all agreed to reduce the amount of workload.
(3) Mr. Peter raised the staff's recent complaints: product supply has lagged sales.
(4) Miss Kate pointed out that the problem was caused by the lack of workers.
(5) Miss Janet proposed to employ more workers and further optimize the production flow.
2. Information of next meeting
Mr. Hunter concluded the meeting, and declared that next meeting would be held in Room 806 at 3:00 p.m. on July 25 (Friday).

3. Adjournment

Mr. Hunter adjourned this meeting at 5:00 p.m.

Minutes-taker: Janet, Secretary

Signature: Hunter, Chairperson

Sample 2: Minutes of Marketing Department

Minutes of Marketing Department

Date: September 12, Wednesday

Time: 10:00 a.m.

Venue: Room 708

Present: Albert, Frank, Kevin, Nelson, Philip, Tracy (Secretary)

Apologies for absence: Richard

Chairperson: Susan

The regular weekly meeting of Guangzhou Evergreen Shoes Co., Ltd. was held at 10:00 a.m. on September 12, Wednesday in Room 708. The meeting was presided over by Miss Susan.

Minutes

The minutes of last meeting was approved by all.

New proposal

Mr. Albert reported the sales strategy for next quarter and his proposal was unanimously accepted.

Resolution

1. Miss Susan announced a resolution of Board of Directors that Mr. Frank was appointed as sales manager.

2. Mr. Nelson announced a resolution that a new sales branch would be established in New York on October 5.

Information of next meeting

The next meeting will be held at 9:00 a.m. on September 18, Tuesday and the venue is to be determined.

Adjournment

The meeting was adjourned at 11:30 a.m.

Taken by: Tracy (Secretary)

Confirmed by: Susan (Chairperson)

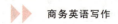

Sample 3: Minutes of Updating Company Profile

Minutes of Updating Company Profile

Date: March 22, Monday

Time: 9:00 a.m.

Place: Room 306

Attendees: Mr. Robert, Mr. Martin, Mr. Peterson, Miss Daisy (Secretary)

Absentee: Mr. Colin

Chairperson: Mr. Edwin

Items:

1. Mr. Edwin in the chair opened the meeting at 9:00 a.m.

2. The minutes of last meeting (March 16) were read by Miss Daisy and approved by all.

3. Issues discussed

(1) Mr. Robert stated that some new photos should be posted on the company profile to make it more vivid.

(2) Mr. Martin advised that the text should be further revised and checked carefully before printing.

(3) Mr. Peterson proposed that the layout might be beautified further to attract customers' attention.

4. Mr. Edwin concluded the meeting, and declared the time, date and place of next meeting and the adjournment of this meeting.

Time, date and place of next meeting:

March 29, Monday, 9:00 a.m.

Place:

To be announced

Adjournment:

11:00 a.m.

Taken by: Miss Daisy, Secretary

Signed by: Mr. Edwin, Chairperson

 Sample Structure

1. Head/Title

2. Date, time and place

3. Attendees

4. Absentees

> 5. Chairperson
> 6. Items
> 7. Information of next meeting
> 8. Adjournment
> 9. Minutes-taker
> 10. Signature

Structure Analysis

1. Head/Title: To state the subject matter of minutes and it usually writes as follows.

> Minutes, MINUTES, Minutes of Marketing Meeting

2. Date, time and place: To state the date, time and where the meeting was held.

> Date: July 17, Thursday
> Time: 3:00 p.m.
> Place: Room 403

3. Attendees: To state the persons who were present at the meeting.

> Attendees: Mr. Mark, Mr. Peter, Miss Kate, Miss Janet (Secretary)

4. Absentees: To state the persons who were absent from the meeting.

> Absentee: Mr. Black

5. Chairperson: To state by whom the meeting was chaired or hosted.

> Chairperson: Mr. Hunter

6. Items: To list the main topics or issues discussed, proposed, declared or decided during the meeting in order; it is the most important part.

> **Items**
> (1) Mr. Hunter read the minutes of the meeting of July 8 and all approved it.
> (2) Mr. Mark reported on overtime work, and all agreed to reduce the amount of workload.
> (3) Mr. Peter raised the issue of recent staff complaints: product supply has lagged sales.
> ...

7. Information of next meeting: To state the date, time and where the next meeting will be held.

Date, time and place of next meeting:
July 25, Friday
Time: 3:00 p.m.
Room 806

8. Adjournment: To state what time the meeting was finished.

The meeting adjourned at 5:00 p.m.

9. Minutes-taker: To state by whom the minutes were taken; to keep them objective and authentic, and handwritten signature is preferred.

Minutes-taker: Janet, Secretary

10. Signature: To state by whom the minutes was confirmed; to keep them objective and authentic, and handwritten signature is preferred.

Signature: Hunter, Chairperson

 Writing Tips

1. Be concise and clear. As a tool of efficient internal communication, minutes should be concise. You can only summarize what actually happened in the meeting.

2. Use formal words and passive voice. As the minutes are used to keep the record of the meetings, formal words and passive voice are frequently used.

3. Be focused. Effective minutes usually discuss a single topic; thus the readers may concentrate on that subject.

4. Be objective. The minutes should keep exactly the record of what actually happened during the meeting.

5. Prepare your meeting minutes outline based on the meeting agenda and follow the order in which the topics were discussed.

6. Keep the minutes short and to the point. Don't waffle and if you want to record every word said, you might consider a tape recording to supplement the minutes.

7. Don't wait too long to write the minutes, especially while your memory is fresh, preferably within 48 hours. Get approval from the chairperson before distributing them.

8. Remember the minutes only need to record the essence of the important discussions. All other information should be excluded from it.

Useful Expressions

1. A meeting was held in Room 306 at 2:15 p.m. today to discuss the sales problems.
今天下午2:15在306室召开了会议,讨论销售问题。

2. The attendants/Those present included all staff of marketing department.
出席会议者包括营销部门全体人员。

3. Apologies (Absence) were (was) received from Peter.
皮特没有出席。

4. The meeting was called to order by Jane at 10:30 a.m.
上午10:30,珍妮宣布会议正式开始。

5. Minutes of the meeting held at 2:00 p.m. on May 20 were approved by all.
大家一致通过了5月20日下午2:00召开的会议纪要。

6. It was decided by unanimous vote to recommend the purchase of Lenovo laptop computers.
与会者一致通过决议,推荐购买联想笔记本电脑。

7. Secretary Lucy is required to make a cost comparison of buying new equipment versus repairing the old one, and it is to be discussed at next meeting.
秘书露西务必将购买新设备和维修旧设备的费用做一个对比,以便下次会议讨论。

8. It is suggested that a new system of quality control should be introduced and installed for the sake of improving product quality.
为了提高产品质量,建议引进并安装一套新的质控系统。

9. Chairman announced/declared that Cathy had been elected Marketing Manager.
主席宣布凯茜当选为市场部经理。

10. The chairperson introduced a new motion, which was passed by unanimous vote.
主席提出了一项新的议案,大家一致表决通过。

11. There were 15 affirmative votes, 3 negative votes and 1 abstention.
15张赞成票,3张反对票,1张弃权票。

12. The next regular meeting is scheduled at 2:30 p.m. on May 15.
下次例会安排在5月15日下午2:30。

13. The next meeting will be held at 9:00 a.m. on September 18, Tuesday and the venue is to be determined.
下次会议将于9月18日(星期二)上午9:00举行,地点待定。

14. The meeting was adjourned (ended) at 4:15 p.m.
会议于下午4:15结束。

15. The minutes were taken and submitted to the general manager by Secretary Ellen.
会议记录由秘书艾伦整理并提交给总经理。

16. The minutes were confirmed and signed to be true and accurate record of the meeting proceeding by Chairman Mr. Hilton.

会议记录经董事长希尔顿先生确认并签名,证实为真实准确的会议过程记录。

Task Solving

After studying what has been presented above, you may know how to compose minutes successfully.

Consolidation Exercise

1. Please fill in the blanks according to the initial letter.

Minutes of the Company's Seminar on Technology Innovation and Development

Date: January 5
Time: 9:00 a.m.-11:00 a.m.
Place: Room 1016, Innovation Building
Attendee: Mr. Wang Dali, Mr. Li He, Ms. Zhang Guotao, Mr. Hu Jinli, Miss Ma Li
Absentee: Mr. Chen Dong (Illness)
Chairperson: Mr. Wang Dali
1. The minutes of last meeting (December 23) were read and (1) a_____ by all.
2. Participants had in-depth discussion on the current challenges and opportunities in the (2) f_____ of technology (3) i_____ and development.
3. Participants agreed that the development of new products is (4) e_____ for the company's long-term growth and competitiveness.
4. Participants also discussed the importance of (5) p_____ improvement and innovation in enhancing the company's operational efficiency and (6) r_____ costs.
5. Participants identified several trends that are shaping the industry, including the growing demand for (7) p_____ products and services, the rise of e-commerce, etc.
6. Participants proposed several strategies, including (8) i_____ investment in research and development, and (9) f_____ a culture of innovation within the organization.
7. Mr. Wang Dali (10) c_____ the meeting and declared the date, time and place of next meeting and the adjournment of this meeting.

Date, time and place of next meeting: January 12, Room 1016, Innovation Building
Adjournment: 11:00 a.m.
Signature: Mr. Wang Dali
Minutes taken by: Miss Ma Li

2. Please translate the English underlined into Chinese.

Minutes of Expanding the Capacity of the Sunlight Company

Date: September 8 (Friday)
Time: 9:00 a.m.
Place: Room 707, Floor 10, Sunlight Company
Attendees:
Miss Aanna (Production Manager)
Mr. Blair (Procurement Manager)
Mr. Charlie (Finance Manager)
Mr. Dan (Office Director)
Miss Emily (Secretary to General Manager)
Chairperson: Mr. John (General Manager)

1. The minutes of the last meeting were read and (1) <u>approved by vote, with one negative vote and two abstentions.</u>
2. Details of this meeting
• Miss Aanna (Production Manager) (2) <u>put forward her goal to increase the annual production capacity by 20%</u> within the next six months by improving production processes and improving equipment efficiency.
• Mr. Blair (Procurement Manager) was committed to (3) <u>ensuring to obtain a stable and high-quality supply of raw materials</u> for the production department so that the company's goal for expanding production capacity can be achieved.
• Mr. Charlie (Finance Manager) developed a detailed budget ensuring (4) <u>our capacity expansion plan economically sustainable</u> including a comprehensive analysis of required capital, cost-effectiveness, expected returns, and risks.
• Mr. Dan (Office Director) promised to review and (5) <u>optimize the existing office processes and improve work efficiency</u> in support of the capacity expansion plan.
3. Summary
Mr. John (General Manager) made a summary of the meeting, announced the time, date and place of next meeting, and adjourned the meeting.
4. Time, date and place of next meeting
2:30 p.m., September 15 (Friday); Room 609, Floor 6
5. Adjournment
11:00 a.m.

Minutes-taker: Miss Emily, Secretary to General Manager
Signed by: Mr. John, Chairperson

3. Please translate the Chinese in the brackets into English.

Minutes of New Product Designing Committee
Date: December 12, Tuesday
Time: 2:30 p.m.
Place: Room 508
Present: Austin (Chairperson), Benjamin (Chief Designer), Henry, James, All salespersons, Aimee (Secretary)
Apologies: Michael
Items:
1. _____(奥斯丁宣读上次会议的记录并获得一致通过).
2. _____(首席设计师本杰明用图片展示了新设计的汽车). He explained the advantages of the new car.
3. Henry put forward his advice on the new design. He thought that the new car was better than the previous model and _____(更容易被国内外的客户接受).
4. The presenters discussed whether the new car would be launched in the European market. The result is 3 affirmative votes, 1 negative vote and 0 abstention. Austin requested that _____(全体销售人员调查新车在欧洲市场受接受的程度).
5. James proposed to study the similar products from other car companies and modify the design further as soon as possible.
6. _____(奥斯丁总结了本次会议并宣布下次会议的时间和地点) and adjourned the meeting.
Date, time and place of next meeting:
9:30 a.m., December 19, Tuesday, Room 406
Adjournment:
5:30 p.m.
Taken by: Aimee, Secretary
Confirmed by: Austin, Chairperson

Writing Practice

Directions: Supposing you are Jennifer as a secretary working in Guangzhou Pacific Trading Company. Mr. Vincent (Chairperson) is hosting a meeting discussing the issue of opening new branches overseas. The meeting is being held in Room 1206 at 2:30 p.m. on May 25, Friday. Mr. Angus (Marketing Manager), Mr. George, Mr. Daniel, Tina and you are present, but Miss Shelly is absent for business trip. Please write minutes according to the following issues discussed in the meeting.

> **Vincent:**
> Well, everyone is here. Shall we start? As you know, we are having this meeting to discuss whether it is the right time to expand our business, particularly whether we should open more branches overseas. Angus, since you are the marketing manager, perhaps you can briefly introduce the situation first.
>
> **Angus:**
> Yes. I have been looking at our sales figures from the past few years, and it seems to me that we should set up new branches in new areas where there is a great demand for our products.
>
> **George:**
> Sorry to interrupt. I think you are a bit quick with your conclusion there. I have a different interpretation of the situation. Personally speaking, I am in favor of expanding our present branches rather than setting up new ones. Please think of the cost of risking new ventures in new places with new overheads.
>
> **Daniel:**
> Excuse me, George. I would like to break in here. I think you are over-pessimistic. I agree with you that we have to spend on facilities, staff training, advertising and so on. But Angus is right because the demand is there. Maybe Tina can tell you something about Shenzhen Sunshine Shoes Company.
>
> **Tina:**
> Yes. I was going to mention that. The day before yesterday, I overheard from a friend that Shenzhen Sunshine Shoes Company is planning to expand their business in England. I mean, if we don't grasp the opportunity, our competitors will. Don't you think so?
>
> **George:**
> Well. I still stick to my point. I think it is more advisable to upgrade our present facilities and postpone opening new branches.
>
> **Tina:**
> Well, everyone knows the saying "Time is money". If we miss the opportunity, our rivals will take over the market. And I do think it is necessary to open new branches.
>
> **Vincent:**
> All right. I feel we have discussed this matter fully. You have made some valuable points and suggestions. To sum up, there are strong reasons for opening new branches

overseas next year. I will present your ideas to the board of directors. Is there any other business? No? Okay, that's all for today. I would like to conclude by thanking you all for your time and contributions. I will tell you as soon as I get a response from the board of directors. By the way, the time, date and place of next meeting is at 2:30 p.m. on June 1, Friday in Room 1206. It is 5:00 p.m. I declare this meeting is over.

Module 3 Writing for Publicizing and Advertising

Task 1 Announcement

Learning Objectives

- Learn about the definition, function and types of announcement.
- Be familiar with the structure, content and format of announcement.
- Master the useful expressions such as words, phrases and sentences of announcement.
- Be able to skillfully compose a correct announcement in the real business situation.

Task Situation

To express thanks for the support and help of its customers and friends at home and abroad, Guangzhou Fortune Trade Company is going to celebrate its 20th anniversary on July 7. Mr. Stephen tells Mabel to compose a public announcement and have it posted on the company's website so that it is known to all staff, customers and friends. The details of the announcement are as follows.

> Subject: Announcement of Guangzhou Fortune Trade Company's 20th Anniversary
> Time and Date: 9:00 a.m.-5:30 p.m., July 7 (Friday)
> Place: Banquet Hall, Floor 18, Guangzhou Garden Hotel
> Participants: All staff, customers and friends at home and abroad
> Date of composing the announcement: June 8

Supposing you are Mabel, how do you finish the task assigned to you?

Questions

- What basic contents are included in an announcement?
- How are the structure and format of an announcement?
- What points should we pay attention to when composing an announcement?

Theory Background

The announcement, a short written or printed sheet, which is mainly used for external communication (i.e. compared with "notice" mainly dealing with internal communication), displays information to the public. It is usually published in newspapers, posted in public places or sent as letters or e-mails.

The announcement is widely used in many business occasions. It can be used to advertise a new product or service, to announce opening a new branch, to establish a subsidiary, and to merge companies, etc.

According to its content, announcement can be classified into different types, such as announcement of establishing a new branch, announcement of removal, announcement of new products, announcement of new branch opening, announcement of companies' merging, announcement of temporarily closing business, announcement of name change, announcement of price increase, etc.

 ## Sample Study

Sample 1: Announcement of establishing a new branch

Announcement of Establishing a New Branch

April 5

Dear Sir or Madam,

Owing to the large increase in the volume of our trade with Guangzhou, we have decided to open a branch here. Mr. Wilson will work as the sales manager. The new branch will be open on April 15 and from that date all orders from Guangzhou should be sent to Mr. Wilson at the following e-mail instead of our Shenzhen branch.

We take this opportunity to express our sincere thanks for your cooperation in the past several years.

Lotus Foreign Trade Company
Add: 188 Huangpu Avenue, Guangzhou
E-mail: lotusgz@sina.com.cn
Tel: 020-××××　××××
Fax: 020-××××　××××

Sample 2: Announcement of removal

> **Announcement of Removal**
>
> Owing to the speedy expansion of our business, we find it is necessary to remove our company to more spacious premises.
>
> We are glad to inform you that our company will be removed to No. 168, Tianhe North Road, Guangzhou on and after March 1.
>
> You are warmly welcome to our new premises.
>
> Peak Sports Clothing Co., Ltd.
Tel: 020-××××　××××

Sample 3: Announcement of company name change

> **Announcement of Company Name Change**
>
> Dear Customers,
>
> We have recently changed the name of our company from Guangzhou Kelvin Co., Ltd. to Guangzhou Karl Co., Ltd. from now on. There has been no change in our address, products and services and we will always provide the same fine products and good services on which we have built our reputation in the industry.
>
> We would be highly appreciated if you could tell this announcement to the people around you. We are looking forward to your visit.
>
> Guangzhou Karl Co., Ltd.
Tel: 020-××××　××××

Sample 4: Announcement of temporarily closing business

> **Announcement of Spring Festival Holiday**
>
> Our online shop will be temporarily closed from 6:00 p.m., January 31 (Wednesday) to 7:00 a.m., February 12 (Monday).
>
> Enjoy your holiday!
>
> Guangzhou Bright Color Cosmetics Co., Ltd.
Tel: 020-××××　××××

Sample Structure

> 1. Head/Title
> 2. Date
> 3. Body
> 4. Company/Organization
> 5. Contact way

 Structure Analysis

A public announcement does not have a fixed layout. It varies for different messages, but the following parts are always necessary.

1. Head/Title: To state the subject matter of announcement or just write the usual title "announcement", located on the top.

> Announcement of Establishing a New Branch

2. Date: To state the issuing time of the announcement, usually located in the left top corner.

> April 5

3. Body: To state the main content such as the activity, the time, the place, and other details.

> Owing to the large increase in the volume of our trade with Guangzhou, we have decided to open a branch here. Mr. Wilson will work as the sales manager...

4. Company/Organization: To show by which company, organization or institution the announcement is issued.

> Lotus Foreign Trade Company

5. Contact way: To provide the means of contacting such as person, address, telephone, fax, e-mail, website, etc.

> Add: No. 188, Huangpu Avenue, Guangzhou
> Email: lotusgz@sina.com.cn
> Tel: 020-×××× ××××
> Fax: 020-×××× ××××

Writing Tips

1. Be brief, clear and complete.
2. Use sub-headings to break up the main information into small paragraphs.
3. Use asterisks or numerals to mark important information.
4. Highlight headings and important information by using typographical devices such as capitals, bold, underlining, or italics.
5. Ask someone to double-check your spelling and general content.

Useful Expressions

1. It is hereby proclaimed that the board of directors has voted to dismiss Mr. Thomas from the position of president.

公司董事会已投票决定免除托马斯先生的主席职务,特此通知。

2. We have the pleasure to declare that Miss Lily has been elected as the department manager.

我们很高兴地宣布,莉莉女士当选为部门经理。

3. We are honored to announce that Mr. Henry has been promoted to senior vice president of the sales department.

我们很荣幸地宣布,亨利先生晋升为销售部高级副总裁。

4. We are pleased to take the opportunity to announce that the sales department and the marketing department have been merged together.

我们很高兴地借此机会宣布,本公司的销售部门和营销部门已合并。

5. We are pleased to inform you that our business will be turned into a limited company on July 1.

本公司将于7月1日改为有限公司,特此通知。

6. We hereby inform you that our factory has moved to the following address.

本厂已迁往下列地址,特此通知。

7. Because of the fast growth of our business, we find it necessary to move our company to a more central area.

由于业务的快速增长,公司需要搬迁到更中心的区域。

8. Owning to the needs for business expansion, our company has merged with Wilson Trade Company under the name of Oriental Trading Group.

由于业务拓展的需要,我公司以东方贸易集团的名义与威尔逊贸易公司合并。

9. You are warmly welcome to visit our new office.

热忱欢迎阁下光临我公司新办事处。

10. On and after April 2, our company will be moved to Guangzhou Pazhou International Convention and Exhibition Center. 自4月2日起，本公司将搬迁到广州琶洲国际会展中心。

11. We inform you that we shall move to Zhujiang New Town on August 8.
我们将于8月8日搬到珠江新城，特此通知。

12. We sincerely hope that the establishment of new branch will offer you higher standards in the service.
我们衷心希望新分公司的成立将会为您们提供更高标准的服务。

13. The owner is expected to come to Room 311, Administrative Building to claim the lost bag.
请失主到行政楼311室认领丢失的包。

14. The owner should get in contact with Miss Cathy.
请失主与凯西女士联系。

 Task Solving

After studying what has been presented above, you may know how to compose an announcement successfully.

 Consolidation Exercise

1. Please fill in the blanks according to the initial letter.

ANNOUNCEMENT

Dear customers,

　　We are excited to (1) a_____ that towards the end of this year, Sunshine will be hosting a (2) s_____ of promotional activities at the Sun City Plaza. The event is set to take place at the plaza's (3) p_____ location, ensuring maximum exposure and convenience for all our valued (4) c_____.

　　The (5) r_____ of products involved in this promotion is extensive and includes a wide (6) v_____ of household appliances designed to make your life (7) e_____. Whether you're looking for a new kettle, toaster, or even a fully-featured (8) k_____ appliance, our selection has something for everyone.

　　We hope to see you at the Sun City Plaza for this exciting event! For more (9) i_____, please visit our website or contact us at 020-××××××××.

　　Thank you for your time and we look forward to the opportunity to (10) s_____ you.

Sunshine Team

2. Please translate the English underlined into Chinese.

Announcement of AITO M9 Launch

November 24

　　We are pleased to announce that TG Rock Company, which is closely cooperating with Grace Corporation, (1) <u>has officially announced the launch plan of its new model</u>—AITO M9. This car is equipped with a newly upgraded Olive Four System and (2) <u>is expected to be launched in the fourth quarter of this year</u>. We are now (3) <u>accepting inquiries and bookings from our new and regular users</u>.

　　The AITO M9 not only (4) <u>inherits the persistent pursuit of high-quality cars</u> from TG Rock, but also demonstrates Grace's deep empowerment in intelligent technology. The Olive Four System of this model has undergone a new upgrade, which will (5) <u>bring a smoother and more functional user experience</u>.

　　If you have any inquiries about this model, please feel free to contact us at any time.

　　Thank you for your continuous attention and support to TG Rock and welcome to enjoy your new journey.

Rock Corporation
Tel: 400-×××　×××
Website: https://www.rock.com

3. Please translate the Chinese in the brackets into English.

Announcement of Establishing a New Branch

　　We are pleased to inform you that ＿＿＿＿＿＿＿＿＿＿＿＿＿＿＿＿＿＿＿＿＿＿＿＿＿＿＿＿＿＿＿＿＿＿＿＿＿(由于我公司发展的需要), we ＿＿(决定成立一家新分公司) at No. 89, Beijing Road, Guangzhou, with Mr. Brown in charge. We wish to ＿＿＿＿＿＿＿＿＿＿＿＿＿＿＿＿＿＿＿＿＿＿＿＿＿＿＿＿＿＿＿＿＿＿＿(借此机会表达我们诚挚的感谢) for your support in the past and ＿＿＿＿＿＿＿＿＿＿＿＿＿＿＿＿＿＿＿＿＿＿＿＿＿＿＿＿(希望新分公司的设立) will give you completely new services.

　　＿＿＿＿＿＿＿＿＿＿＿＿＿＿＿＿＿＿＿＿＿＿＿＿＿＿＿＿＿＿＿＿＿＿＿＿＿＿＿(热忱欢迎大家光临我司新分公司).

L&R Electric Lights Company

🔑 Writing Practice ////

Directions: Shelly works in Brothers Trading Company. Owning to its speedy expansion, her company will be removed to a new address, so her boss asks her to write an announcement, making the following information known to the public.

Date: On and after July 4
New place: No.118, Luhu Road, Guangzhou
New telephone: 020-××××××××
New fax: 020-××××××××

Task 2　Business Card

 Learning Objectives

- Learn about the definition, function and types of business card.
- Be familiar with the structure, content and format of business card.
- Master the useful expressions such as words, phrases and sentences for business card.
- Be able to skillfully compose a correct business card in the real business situation.

 Task Situation

In order to better communicate with others, Mr. Stephen asks Mabel to write and design a business card for him. The basic information is as follows.

Name: Stephen
Title: General Manger
Company name: Guangzhou Fortune Trade Company
Tel: 020-×××× ××××
Fax: 020-×××× ××××
E-mail: gzft@yahoo.com
Website: www.gzft.com
Address: No.196, Tianhe North Road, Guangzhou, China

Supposing you are Mabel, how do you finish the task assigned to you?

 Questions

- What basic contents are included in a business card?
- How are the structure and format of a business card?
- What points should we pay attention to when composing a business card?

 Theory Background

Business cards are physical items that convey professional details regarding a company or an individual. They serve as an aid for easy recollection and convenience during formal introductions. It is mainly used for self-introduction and as ways of keeping in touch with others. The standard elements on a business card include the holder's name, company name and logo, and the contact ways such as postal address, telephone number, fax number, e-mail, and website.

Sample Study

Sample 1: Business card for a sales manager

Mark Wang

Sales Manager

Guangzhou Angel Children's Toy Co., Ltd.

Address: Room 2108, Floor 21, Building A, Xiushui Industrial Park
　　　　 No.36, Renhe North Street, Baiyun District, Guangzhou

Tel: 020-×××× ××××; Fax: 020-×××× ××××

E-mail: markwang@yahoo.com; Website: www.gzangel.com

Business scope: Puzzle toys for children aged 3 to 12

Strong will for long distance and broad mind for holding the world

Sample 2: Business card for a COO

Guo Yongsheng

COO, co-founder

Beijing Ciku Science and Technology, Co., Ltd.

Tel: 158 ×××× ××××; 010-×××× ××××

E-mail: guoyongsheng@ciku.com

Floor 2, Resource Building,

Beijing University of Posts and Telecommunications,

Haidian District, Beijing, China

Sample 3: Business card for a lecturer

Joanne Fleer

Lecturer

Training and Education

Tel: +61(8)×××× ××××

E-mail: joanne.fleer@tafesa.edu.au

Adelaide City Campus

No. 120, Currie Street, Adelaide SA 5000

tafesa.edu.au

Sample 4: Business card for a CEO

Mark Stone

Chief executive officer

Guangzhou Eastern Real Estate Agency Co., Ltd.

Address: No.25, Binjiang East Road
    Haizhu District, Guangzhou, China
Tel: 020-××××　××××
Fax:020-××××　××××

Sample 5: Business card for an individual

JOHN DOE

TEL:020-××××　××××
URL:www.loremipsum.com
E-mail:lorem@ipsum.com

 ## Sample Structure ////

1. Name of business, department or an individual
2. Holder's name
3. Holder's position or title
4. Contact ways such as address, telephone number, e-mail, etc.
5. Other information such as QR codes, logos, photos, etc.

 ## Structure Analysis ////

 1. Name of business, department or an individual: It is usually located in the top middle.

Sinopec Group (中国石油化工集团公司)
China National Petroleum Corporation, CNPC (中国石油天然气集团公司)
State Grid Corporation of China, SGCC (国家电网公司)
Ping An Insurance (Group) Company of China, Ltd.[中国平安保险(集团)股份有限公司]
Industrial and Commercial Bank of China, ICBC (中国工商银行)
Foxconn Technology Group (富士康科技集团)
China Construction Bank, CCB (中国建设银行)
Agricultural Bank of China, ABC (中国农业银行)
China Life Insurance (Group) Company [中国人寿保险(集团)公司]
Huawei Technologies Co., Ltd.(华为技术有限公司)
Alibaba Group Holding Limited (阿里巴巴集团)
Tencent Holdings Limited (腾讯控股有限公司)

2. Holder's name

Tim Cook (蒂姆·库克)
Satya Nadella (萨提亚·纳德拉)
Andy Jassy (安迪·贾西)
Sundar Pichai (桑达尔·皮查伊)
Arvind Krishna (阿尔温德·克里希纳)
Tom Gelsinger (汤姆·基辛格)

3. Holder's position or title

Chief Executive Officer (CEO)(首席执行官)
Chief Operating Officer (COO)(首席运营官)
Chief Financial Officer (CFO)(首席财务官/财务总监)
Chief Technology Officer (CTO)(首席技术官)
Chief Marketing Officer (CMO)(首席营销官)
Chief Information Officer (CIO)(首席信息官)
Chief Human Resources Officer (CHRO)(首席人力资源官)
Chief Legal Officer (CLO)/ General Counsel (GC)(首席法务官/总法律顾问)Chief Strategy Officer (CSO)(首席战略官)
Chief Digital Officer (CDO)(首席数字官)
Chief Product Officer (CPO)(首席产品官)
Chief Risk Officer (CRO)(首席风险官)
Chief Sustainability Officer (CSO)(首席可持续发展官)
Chief Customer Officer (CCO)(首席客户官)

4. Contact ways such as address, telephone number, e-mail, etc.

Apple Park Way, Cupertino, CA 95014, USA (Apple Inc. address)

One Microsoft Way, Redmond, WA 98052-6399, USA(Microsoft Corporation address)

410 Terry Avenue North, Seattle, WA 98109-5210, USA(Amazon.com Inc. address)

3500 Deer Creek Road, Palo Alto, CA 94304, USA(Tesla Inc. address)

Huawei Base, Bantian, Longgang District, Shenzhen, Guangdong Province, China(Huawei Technologies Co., Ltd. address)

No. 580, Guangyuan Middle Road, Baiyun District

---

5. Other information such as QR codes, logos, photos, etc. (optional)

Writing Tips

1. Be brief. Try to include vital information, not all information for highlighting the key parts.

2. Make it memorable. Under this guideline, try using some unique logos, QR codes or photos, even some slogans or mottoes.

3. Make your letter appealing in content and correct in spelling, grammar and facts.

Useful Expressions

1. Chief Executive Officer (CEO) 首席执行官

2. President 总裁

3. Chairman 董事长,主席

4. Vice President (VP)副总裁

5. Manager 经理

6. Supervisor 主管

7. Director 总监

8. Coordinator 协调员

9. Administrator 管理员

10. Executive Assistant (EA)行政助理

11. Office Manager 办公室主任

12. Sales Representative 销售代表
13. Sales Executive 销售主管
14. Customer Service Representative (CSR) 客户服务代表
15. Product Manager 产品经理
16. Human Resources Manager (HRM) 人力资源经理
17. Accountant 会计师
18. Power Plant 发电厂
19. Brewery Plant 啤酒厂
20. Paper Mill 造纸厂
21. Brick Works 砖厂
22. Apple Corporation 苹果公司
23. Shanghai Co., Ltd 上海有限公司
24. Tesla Inc. 特斯拉公司
25. China Southern Airlines 中国南方航空公司
26. SF Express 顺丰快递公司
27. China Youth Travel Service 中国青春旅行社
28. Law Firm 法律事务所
29. Guangzhou Pawnshop 广州典当行

Task Solving

After studying what has been presented above, you may know how to compose a business card successfully.

Consolidation Exercise

1. Please fill in the blanks according to the initial letter.

Mark Liu

General Manager

Guangzhou Golden Trade Company

(1) A_____: No.196, Tianhe North Road, Guangzhou, China

Tel: 020-××××××××; Fax: 020-××××××××

E-mail: gzft@yahoo.com; (2) W_____: www.gzft.com

*Company's (3) P_____:

*We (4) t_____ to provide the highest quality (5) p_____ and services for our customers.

---

* We (6) e_____ teamwork, mutual (7) b_____, and shared success.
* We uphold the (8) p_____ of integrity, innovation and excellence in everything we do.
* We are (9) c_____ to sustainable development and actively (10) f_____ our social responsibilities.

2. Please translate the English underlined into Chinese.

Richard Chen

(1) General Manager, Consumer Business Division
(2) Guangzhou Warwick Technologies Co., Ltd.

☆ Address: (3) Room 1801, Building C, South China Smart Park
　　　　　No.223, Huangpu Avenue, Tianhe District, Guangzhou, China
☆ Tel: 020-××××　××××; Fax: 020-××××　××××
☆ Email: richard@warwick.com; Website: www.gzwarwick.com
☆ (4) Company's Mission: Make communication better
☆ (5) You are welcome for inquiry if you have any ideas.

3. Please translate the Chinese in the brackets into English.

Edward Song

_____(人力资源部高级经理)
_____(广州路易斯跨境电商公司)

☆ Address: Room 2202, Floor 22, City Building, _____
_____(广州南沙自由贸易区)
No.346, Nansha Avenue, Nansha District, Guangzhou, China
☆ Tel: 020-××××　××××; Fax: 020-××××　××××
☆ Email: edwardsong@sina.com; Website: www.gzlouis.com
☆ _____(我们的使命：买全球，卖全球)
☆ _____(一握君之手,永远为朋友)

Writing Practice

Directions: Colin Smith is the sales manager of Atlanta Double Trade Company. Please design an English business card for him based on the following information.

公司：亚特兰大德宝贸易有限公司
地址：No. 128, Baker Street, Atlanta, Georgia, 30313, U.S.A.
电话：＋91 484 ××× ××××
传真：＋91 484 ××× ××××
网址：www.atlantadoubletc.com

Task 3　Company Profile

 Learning Objectives

- Learn about the definition, function and types of company profile.
- Be familiar with the structure, content and format of company profile.
- Master the useful expressions such as words, phrases and sentences for company profile.
- Be able to skillfully compose a correct company profile in the real business situation.

 Task Situation

In order to help customers to better understand the company and meet the need of celebrating its 20th anniversary, Mr. Stephen asks Mabel to revise and update the company profile on the website according to the following details.

Specializing: Mainly dealing with import and export business

Business scope: Garments, shoes, bags, cosmetics, and household appliances

History: Founded in 2004

Location: Guangzhou

Market objective: Customers worldwide

Company's philosophy: Customer foremost and service first

Contact way:

Add: No.196, Tianhe North Road, Guangzhou, China

Tel: 020-××××　××××

Fax: 020-××××　××××

E-mail: gzft@yahoo.com

Website: www.gzft.com

Supposing you are Mabel, how do you finish the task assigned to you?

 Questions

- What basic contents are included in a company profile?
- How are the structure and format of a company profile?
- What points should we pay attention to when composing a company profile?

Theory Background

A company profile is a brief description or introduction of a company. It usually includes the following aspects: location, history, development, scale, and business scope; market objectives or areas, range of products or services; honor, award, company culture, mission, philosophy or policy; contact way.

A good company profile not only provides customers with complete information, but also demonstrates them a good image. Besides, it can also establish trust with the customers and help them to better understand, choose or purchase products or services.

According to its content and function, company profile can be classified into as many different kinds as it can be.

 ## Sample Study

Sample 1

Profile of Guangzhou Sophia Clothes Co., Ltd.

Established in 1994, Guangzhou Sophia Clothes Co., Ltd. is a clothing enterprise specializing in the design, development and production of women's clothes. We are located in Guangzhou Airport Economic Zone with a very convenient transportation.

Covering an area of 80,000 square meters, we now have more than 1,500 employees with a monthly production capacity of 100,000 pieces and an annual sales figure exceeding USD 120 million. We have established a global sales network reaching North America, Europe and East Asia, and currently export 100% of our products worldwide.

Our well-equipped facilities and strict quality control system enable us to make our customers completely satisfied. Besides, we have received a certificate of ISO 9001. All of our products comply with international quality standards and are greatly appreciated in the markets all over the world.

As our products are excellent in quality, we have won "The Most Popular Brand Award" every year since 2015 and become one of the leading brands for women's clothes around the world. Aimee, Daisy and Patty are our three most famous brands.

Sophia has been sticking to the philosophy of "Adhering to Originality" since it was founded. And we also have been devoted to making more beautiful, fashionable and elegant clothes for our customers in the world.

> If you are interested in any of our products or would like to discuss a custom order, please feel free to contact us. We are looking forward to cooperating with you and creating a better future.
>
> Tel: 020-×××× ××××
> Fax: 020-×××× ××××
> Address: No.23, Renhe North Street, Baiyun District, Guangzhou, China
> E-mail: gzsophia@sina.com
> Website: www. gzsophia.com

Sample 2

> ### Profile of Sunlight Electric Appliances, Inc. of Guangzhou
>
> Sunlight Electric Appliances, Inc. of Guangzhou, founded in 1991, has become the world's leading air conditioning company integrating research & development, manufacturing, sales and service. It ranked one of the "Top 500 Chinese Listed Companies" for eight years running by *Fortune* Magazine. Specializing in manufacturing air conditioners, Sunlight presents excellent quality air conditioning products to global consumers.
>
> It now possesses 9 manufacturing bases in Guangzhou (headquarters), Chongqing, Nanjing, Dalian, Pakistan, Malaysia, Russia, Mexico and South Africa with a total of more than 60,000 employees. Sunlight has gained a great reputation in the international air conditioning industry and now is developing from a "Made-in-China" enterprise into a "Created-in-China" one.
>
> Sunlight insists on the notion of "independent development and original innovation brand", and it is ready to produce and innovate more "Created-in-China" products.

Sample 3

> ### South China Textiles Import & Export Group
>
> South China Textiles Import & Export Group is an economic entity with legal status. Its business mainly covers the import and export of textiles.
>
> Our corporation has a staff of 215, occupying a floor area of 80,000 square meters of office. Since founded in 1983 in Guangzhou, we have established good business relationships with over 130 countries and regions around the world and set up branches and offices in Europe, South America, North America and Africa.

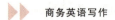

We always follow the principle of "Customers and Reputation Come First" and keep improving and innovating our products. And we sincerely invite both new and regular customers at home and abroad to negotiate business.

Thank you for your interest in our products and please visit our website www. sctextiles. com for further information about our company.

Tel: 020-××××　××××

Fax: 020-××××　××××

Address: No. 176, Beijing Road, Yuexiu District, Guangzhou, Guangdong, China

Website: www. sctextiles.com

E-mail: sctextiles@sina.com

Sample 4

Online Shop Introduction of Guangzhou Brilliant Wig Co., Ltd.

Dear Customers,

Welcome to visit our Online-shop (http://www. ebay.gzwig).

Guangzhou Brilliant Wig Co., Ltd. has been specializing in producing wigs for 18 years and can produce more than 3,000 kinds of wigs with two product lines: synthetic fiber product line and human hair product line.

There are multiple colors to select and please refer to the pictures for detailed information. Our goods have been strictly checked before delivery, and we assure you that the defective goods will be immediately replaced with good ones if you receive them and the losses will be refunded accordingly.

With superior quality, reasonable price and excellent service, our products are welcome with customers all over the world and have been exported to 96 countries and regions so far. More than 8,000 customers have added our store to their "My Favorites".

We have been awarded "Diamond Shop", which means our shop has received more than 50,000 good feedbacks from our customers worldwide.

The latest pictures of the products and relative information are usually updated within 24 hours. We also welcome your ODM orders and OEM orders.

If you have any questions, please contact our customer service center at 020-×××× ×××× or e-mail to guangzhouwig@sina.com. Many thanks for your inquiring about our shop and we are looking forward to your order.

Thank you.

Sample Structure

1. Head/Title
2. History and location
3. Business scale
4. Market area or objectives
5. Company's strengths
6. Honors and awards
7. Business scope and range of products
8. Company culture, mission and philosophy
9. Wishes or expectations
10. Contact way

 Structure Analysis

1. Head/Title: Located in the top middle; it usually writes as follows.

Company profile / COMPANY PROFILE
Profile of Guangzhou Sophia Clothes CO., LTD.

2. History and location: To state how long the company has been founded and where the company is.

Established in 1994, Guangzhou Sophia Clothes Co., Ltd. is a clothing enterprise specializing in the design, development and production of women's clothes. We are located in Guangzhou Airport Economic Zone with a very convenient transportation.

3. Business scale: To state how many employees are hired, how much area is covered and so on.

Covering an area of 80,000 square meters, we now have more than 1,500 employees with a monthly production capacity of 100,000 pieces and an annual sales figure exceeding USD 120 million.

4. Market area or objectives: To state where or to whom your products and service are sold.

We have established a global sales network reaching North America, Europe and East Asia, and currently export 100% of our products worldwide.

5. Company's strengths: To state the company's strengths from the aspects of equipment, management, quality control, etc.

> Our well-equipped facilities and strict quality control system enable us to make our customers completely satisfied. Besides, we have received a certificate of ISO 9001...

6. Honors and awards: To state what honors and awards the company has received.

> As our products are excellent in quality, we have won "The Most Popular Brand Award" every year since 2015 and become one of the leading brands for women's clothes around the world.

7. Business scope and range of products: To state what business or products the company professionally specializes in.

> We are a clothing enterprise specializing in the design, development and production of women's clothes. We have become one of the leading brands for women's clothes around the world. Aimee, Daisy and Patty are our three most famous brands.

8. Company culture, mission and philosophy: To state what culture, mission and philosophy the company stick to.

> Sophia has been sticking to the philosophy of "Adhering to Originality" since it was founded. And we also have been devoted to making more beautiful, fashionable and elegant clothes for our customers in the world.

9. Wishes or expectations: To express your wishes or expectations for customers' cooperation, visit or orders.

> If you are interested in any of our products or would like to discuss a custom order, please feel free to contact us. We are looking forward to cooperating with you and creating a better future.

10. Contact way: To provide the means of contacting such as person, address, telephone, fax, e-mail, website, etc.

> Tel: 020-×××× ××××
> Fax: 020-×××× ××××
> Address: No. 23, Renhe North Street, Baiyun District, Guangzhou, China
> E-mail: guangzhousophia@sina.com
> Website: www.guangzhousophia.com

Writing Tips

1. Be brief. It should be more concise, more convincing, more startling and more to the point that you really want to convey.

2. Be targeted. Organize your information around the purpose and keep your audiences in mind.

3. Use positive, persuasive, interesting and vivid words while be factual on events, which can produce an effective promotion.

4. Be prominent to the characteristics of the products and enclose some pictures of the products, equipment and awards, etc.

5. Focus on the products and services the company offers, which will benefit the readers so as to attract their attention.

 Useful Expressions

1. Established in 1982 and located in Huangpu District, Guangzhou, we are a professional manufacturer and exporter engaged in cosmetics.

本公司创建于1982年,位于广州市黄埔区,是一家专业从事化妆品生产和出口业务的公司。

2. Headquartered in Shenzhen, Huawei Technologies Co., Ltd. employs approximately 207,000 employees in more than 170 countries and regions worldwide.

华为技术有限公司总部设在深圳,在全球170多个国家和地区雇有大约20.7万名员工。

3. Founded in 1891 in Rotterdam, Holland, Royal Philips Electronics Company is a leading manufacturer of lighting and a pioneer in color TV in the world.

皇家飞利浦电子公司1891年成立于荷兰鹿特丹,是世界照明生产商的领头羊,同时也是彩色电视机生产商的先驱。

4. Our company is specializing in the research & development and production of sports shoes, and all of our products comply with international quality standards.

本公司主要从事运动鞋研发与生产业务,所有产品均符合国际质量标准。

5. Our products are greatly appreciated and enjoy a great popularity in different markets throughout the world.

我们的产品在世界各地市场都深受欢迎,并享有很高的声誉。

6. The headquarter of our company is in Shanghai with sales offices all over the world.

本公司总部位于上海,在世界各地设有销售办事处。

7. Our company is one of the leading importers on mobile phones and iPads.

本公司是移动电话和平板电脑的主要进口商之一。

8. Our business scope covers a wide range from healthcare to energy-saving lighting.

本公司的业务范围从医疗保健到节能照明都有涉及。

9. Our plant covers a floor area of 4,500 square meters with Production Department, Sales Department, Quality Control Department and Purchase Department.

我们的工厂占地面积4500平方米,设有生产部、销售部、质检部和采购部。

10. The monthly production capacity of our factory is 200,000 pieces with total annual revenue of USD 30 million.

我们的工厂月生产能力20万件,年总收入3000万美元。

11. Our company mainly provides Asian language services, including translation between English and Chinese, Japanese, Korean, Indonesian, Vietnamese and Thai.

本公司主要提供亚洲区语言服务,包括英语和汉语、日语、韩语、印度尼西亚语、越南语、泰语的互译。

12. We are one of China's largest suppliers of medical equipment with over 30 years' experience in exporting in this industry.

我们是中国最大的医疗设备供货商之一,在本行业拥有30多年的出口经验。

13. Our products are of superior quality, all of which can reach European Import Standards.

我们的产品质量优异,均能达到欧洲进口标准。

14. We accept OEM and ODM orders and we are able to make the goods as per your customized size.

我们接受OEM(原始设备制造商)和ODM(原始设计制造商)订单,可以按照为您定制的尺寸进行生产。

15. The purpose of our corporation is to improve people's lives through continuously technical innovation.

本公司的宗旨是通过持续不断的技术创新改善人们的生活。

16. We are listed on "Top 500 Chinese Enterprises" for eight years running by *Fortune* Magazine.

我们连续八年荣登由《财富》杂志评选的"中国五百强企业"榜单。

17. Our company's philosophy is "Customer Foremost and Service First".

本公司的理念是"客户至上,服务第一"。

18. If you are interested in our products or would like to discuss a custom order, please feel free to contact us.

如果您对我们的产品感兴趣,或有意洽谈订单,请随时联系我们。

19. We will, as always, provide all the new and regular customers with high quality products and excellent services.

我们将一如既往地为所有的新老客户提供优质的产品和出色的服务。

20. Many thanks for your inquiring about our hotel and we are looking forward to the opportunity to serve you.

本酒店非常感谢您的垂询,希望有机会为您服务。

21. Thank you again for your interest in our products and please visit our website for further information about our company.

再次感谢您对本公司产品的关注,如欲了解本公司详情,请登录我们的网站。

22. We are looking forward to cooperating with customers worldwide to create a better future.

我们期待与全球客户携手合作,共创美好未来。

 Task Solving

After studying what has been presented above, you may know how to compose a company profile successfully.

 Consolidation Exercise

1. Please fill in the blanks according to the initial letter.

Guardian Corporation: A Global Leader in Home Appliances

Guardian Corporation, a leading enterprise group worldwide (1) f_____ twenty years ago, has grown into a large-scale conglomerate with 5,000 employees and an annual production (2) v_____ of 200 million yuan. The company is (3) h_____ in Guangzhou, located at No.28, Guangzhou Avenue.

Guardian's primary focus is the production of home appliances, with products (4) s_____ in over 150 countries and regions worldwide.

Guardian Corporation's team is (5) c_____ of highly qualified professionals with 20% employees (6) h_____ postgraduate degree in technology-related fields. This (7) d_____ to technological expertise ensures the company's continued (8) l_____ in the field of home appliances.

Guardian Corporation is (9) d_____ to providing high-quality home appliances that meet the needs of its customers worldwide. With a focus on innovation and technology, the company (10) s_____ to create products that enhance the lives of its users.

Contact information:
Phone: 020-××××　××××
Email: guardian@yahoo.com
Website: www.guardian.com

2. Please translate the English underlined into Chinese.

Company Profile of Angle Corporation

(1) <u>Angle Corporation is officially established in April 2010</u>, and is a consumer electronics and intelligent manufacturing company (2) <u>with a focus on smartphones, intelligent hardware, and AIoT platforms</u> (Artificial Intelligence and Internet of Things).

Since its inception, Angle has become one of the leading global smartphone brands, (3) <u>consistently ranking among the top three global smartphone shippers</u>, and has established a global leading consumer-grade AIoT platform. On December 31, 2022, (4) <u>the group's business has entered over 100 countries and regions worldwide</u>.

Angle's mission is to always adhere to the principle of (5) <u>creating "products that move the hearts of people and have a fair price"</u>, allowing everyone around the world to enjoy the benefits of technology-driven life.

3. Please translate the Chinese in the brackets into English.

Guangzhou Sunshine Garment Company

Guangzhou Sunshine Garment Company is a modern garment company. _____（依靠独特的营销战略及丰富的资源）, our company has become a professional garment manufacturer in the highly competitive markets.

Our company occupies a producing land of 80,000 square meters _____（拥有12套从德国进口的现代化设备）and our annual production capacity is about 1,200,000 pieces. _____（全国各地有300多家专卖店）, selling our own brand "Sunshine" garments, and our products are very popular with people of all ages.

_____（本公司的理念是"用优异的质量创造美好的明天"）. With a professional team engaging in research and development, we are strong at designing the most fashionable colors and styles. Also we have a very strict quality control system to supervise all the production lines.

In the new century, _____（我们将把满足客户需求作为己任）. We sincerely invite you to contact us for further information.

Writing Practice

Directions: Suppose you are a secretary in China International Travel Service Company (CITSC). One day, you are asked to revise the company profile so that customers can better understand your company. The hints are as follows.

> Company name: China International Travel Service Company (CITSC)
> Position: Zhujiang New Town, Guangzhou
> History: Established in 1984
> Business scope: Tour service, hotel, motor coach and cruise operations, ticket agent for domestic and international airlines and railways
> Principle: "Guest Foremost, Quality First"

Task 4　Product Introduction

 Learning Objectives

• Learn about the definition, function and types of product introduction.
• Be familiar with the structure, content and format of product introduction.
• Master the useful expressions such as words, phrases and sentences for product introduction.
• Be able to skillfully compose a product introduction in the real business situation.

 Task Situation

In order to help customers better understand the upcoming products, Mr. Stephen asks Mabel to write and design a product introduction and then send them in the form of letter. The basic information is as follows.

> Product name: Fair and Lovely Natural Organic Lipsticks
>
> Product benefits: "buy one, get one free" offer for this month; get your best lipstick color and rest assured of excellent results.
>
> Product features: natural ingredients like oils, herbs and others; diverse colors keeping your lips in natural color and soft.
>
> Social proof: pass all the tests; give positive feedback.
>
> Call to action: contact us on info@fair&lovely.com; find the pamphlet attached with more information.

Supposing you are Mabel, how do you finish the task assigned to you?

 Questions

• What basic contents are included in a product introduction?
• How are the structure and format of a product introduction?
• What points should we pay attention to when composing a product introduction?

 Theory Background

Product introduction, also called product launch, refers to the initial presentation or explanation of a new product, service, or production process to potential customers, clients, investors, or other stakeholders. It typically includes detailed information about the features, benefits, and unique selling points of the offering, as well as how it differs from competitors' products or services.

It is a business process through which a new product is launched, debuted or published in the market for general users and/or businesses.

A product introduction gives relevant information about the product to potential and existing customers to make them curious to try the product and to market it. It can be used to extend an invitation for a business proposal with a potential customer.

Sample Study

Sample 1

Ultra-Bright Mini LED Flashlight

Our flashlight will illuminate your adventures with the ultra-compact, ultra-bright LED.

With it, you will experience brightness like never before with our high-powered LED technology, and feel secure and prepared for any situation with a dependable lighting companion.

Crafted with precision in Zhejiang Province, this portable light source incorporates ultra-bright LED technology to deliver maximum illumination. Its rechargeable feature is supported by a powerful 18350 lithium-ion battery, ensuring long-lasting use without frequent replacements or charges. Whether you're traversing unfamiliar terrain or simply need a dependable light source, its capability to illuminate great distances makes it an essential tool for outdoor activities. What's more, the device features a modern Type-C charging port, and water resistance, which makes it ideal for outdoor adventures such as hiking, patrolling, night riding, camping, and providing general nighttime illumination.

Trusted by outdoor enthusiasts and professionals around the globe, our flashlight has earned its place as an indispensable companion for any adventure. It has amassed countless positive reviews and testimonials, solidifying its reputation and allowing you to make your choice with unwavering confidence.

It is time to order now and experience the difference our flashlight can make in your outdoor explorations. Don't miss this opportunity to illuminate your path and feel secure in any situation.

Light up your world with the power of mini.

Sample 2

A Self-rescue Tool in Times of Danger—Car Window Breaker

Our car window breaker can quickly break the window glass and provide a passage for passengers to escape in emergency situations. In addition to being used to break car windows, our car window breaker is designed to be portable and lightweight and also can be used to cut seat belts in an emergency if you're involved in a car accident.

The car window breaker features rapid and effortless glass shattering, user-friendly design, robust safety measures, multi-functionality, and portability for emergency escapes. It is easy to operate and made of high-strength materials with sufficient hardness and toughness, which can easily break the car window glass without much trouble. In addition, our car window breaker is also equipped with safety protection device, such as safety switch to prevent accidental contact, further improving the safety of use.

The car window breaker has gained significant social proof through positive reviews and testimonials from satisfied users worldwide. Its effectiveness in emergency situations has been widely recognized, establishing it as a reliable and lifesaving tool in the automotive industry.

Every second is crucial in emergency situations. Choose our car window breaker to provide you and your family with a safety guarantee.

Always right to make safety your essential companion for travel.

Sample 3

Murphy Mosquito-Repellent Toilet Water: Your Summertime Guardian

With its unique blend of herbal essences, Murphy Mosquito-Repellent Toilet Water not only keeps mosquitoes away for up to 7 hours but also offers a refreshing and invigorating experience. It's enriched with precious ingredients like artificial bezoar, artificial musk, and snake's gallbladder extract, making it the perfect companion for your outdoor adventures.

Loved by millions, this formula is proved to be effective, with users reporting fewer mosquito bites and a cooler, more comfortable summer.

Take your phone and contact us right now. For more information, refer to our customer service, and enjoy the natural bliss of Murphy Toilet Water.

Murphy will give you a five-star summer.

Sample 4

Unparalleled Horse Brand Sports Shoes

Discover the perfect blend of comfort and style with Horse Brand Sports Shoes.

These shoes offer unparalleled breathability, keeping your feet fresh and odor-free throughout the day. The ultra-fine fiber upper material ensures a snug fit while the synthetic rubber outsole provides exceptional wear resistance and anti-slip properties.

As a testament to their quality, Horse Brand Sports Shoes have been a favorite among young people in the Pearl River Delta region from 2021 to 2024. Join the movement and experience the difference with a pair of Horse Brand Sports Shoes today. Step into comfort, style, and confidence.

We invite you to experience the exceptional comfort. With a limited-time discount of 10%, this is an opportunity not to be missed. Visit our website at www.horsebrandshoes.com to learn more.

Horse Brand—Your Journey, Our Shoes.

 Sample Structure

1. Headline/Title
2. Product benefits
3. Product features
4. Social proof
5. Call to action
6. Short but powerful slogan

 Structure Analysis

1. Headline/Title: When creating headlines for a product introduction, it's important to focus on the benefits or unique selling points of the product.

Ultra-Bright Mini LED Flashlight
A Self-rescue Tool in Times of Danger—Car Window Breaker
Sunshine Brand Solar Energy-Saving Lamp
Unparalleled Horse Brand Sports Shoes
The X-Phone Pro: Get 24-Hour Battery Life and a Revolutionary Camera

2. Product benefits: This part should highlight the specific benefits and value that the prod-

uct can bring to users or consumers, especially more focused on explaining them from the user's perspective.

> With it, you will experience brightness like never before with our high-powered LED technology, and feel secure and prepared for any situation with a dependable lighting companion.
>
> Our car window breaker can quickly break the window glass and provide a passage for passengers to escape in emergency situations.
>
> It is a revolution in eco-friendly lighting. This lamp offers unparalleled energy efficiency, reducing your carbon footprint and saving your money on electricity bills.
>
> These shoes offer unparalleled breathability, keeping your feet fresh and odor-free throughout the day.

3. Product features: A product feature is a quality or a function of a product. It includes the size, pattern, color, quality, durability, design, possible uses, technical details, etc.

> Its rechargeable feature is supported by a powerful 18350 lithium-ion battery, ensuring long-lasting use without frequent replacements or charges.
>
> The car window breaker features rapid and effortless glass shattering, user-friendly design, robust safety measures, multi-functionality, and portability for emergency escapes.
>
> With a wide illumination range, easy installation, and remote control switch, it's the perfect lighting solution.
>
> The ultra-fine fiber upper material ensures a snug fit while the synthetic rubber outsole provides exceptional wear resistance and anti-slip properties.

4. Social proof: When customers visit online stores, they often tend to prefer products with numerous positive reviews due to uncertainty about their purchase. This is the social proof effect.

> Trusted by outdoor enthusiasts and professionals around the globe, our flashlight has earned its place as an indispensable companion for any adventure. It has amassed countless positive reviews and testimonials.
>
> The car window breaker has gained significant social proof through positive reviews and testimonials from satisfied users worldwide.
>
> Popular with thousands of people as a consistent best-seller for years, this lamp is a testament to quality and reliability.
>
> As a testament to their quality, Horse Brand Sports Shoes have been a favorite among young people in the Pearl River Delta region from 2021 to 2024.

5. Call to action: It encourages readers to take action, such as purchasing products, contacting sales representatives, or visiting company websites. An effective call to action should be clear, direct, and closely linked to the interests and needs of readers.

> It is time to order now and experience the difference our flashlight can make in your outdoor explorations. Don't miss this opportunity to illuminate your path and feel secure in any situation.
>
> Every second is crucial in emergency situations. Choose our car window breaker to provide you and your family with a safety guarantee.
>
> Don't wait; kindly invite you to illuminate your world with Sunshine Brand's Solar Energy-Saving Lamp today by visiting our online shop right now!
>
> We invite you to experience the exceptional comfort. With a limited-time discount of 10%, this is an opportunity not to be missed. Visit our website at www.horsebrandshoes.com to learn more.

6. Short but powerful slogan: A slogan can effectively summarize the core advantages of a product. This part should usually be concise, easy to remember, and able to convey the unique selling points or value proposition of the product.

> Light up your world with the power of mini.
> Always right to make safety your essential companion for travel.
> Murphy will give you a five-star summer.
> Horse Brand—Your Journey, Our Shoes.

Writing Tips

1. Define your target audience. Before writing, conduct research to understand your target audience's needs, interests, and potential concerns, which will help you tailor your message and make your product introduction more relevant and engaging.

2. Highlight unique features and benefits. Emphasize the unique aspects of your product and how it meets your customers' needs. Clearly list the product's features and benefits, and provide supporting data or evidence such as market research results or customer feedback.

3. Use professional language. Maintain a professional tone and adhere to industry standards when writing. Using correct terminology will enhance the credibility of your product and demonstrate your knowledge of the industry.

4. Include a clear call to action and slogan. Conclude your letter with a clear call to action,

encouraging the reader to take the next step, such as visiting your website, contacting you for more information, or purchasing the product.

 Useful Expressions

1. Our product stands out in competition due to innovation and outstanding value.
我们产品因为创新和价值卓越而在竞争中脱颖而出。

2. Our smartphones are meticulously crafted, keeping in mind the diverse needs and interests of our esteemed audience, ensuring a seamless and personalized user experience.
我们的智能手机制作精良,考虑到我们尊敬的受众的不同需求和兴趣,确保了无缝和个性化的用户体验。

3. By addressing potential concerns with cutting-edge technology and user-friendly features, our devices aim to elevate your digital interactions, making every moment more engaging and efficient.
我们的设备通过前沿技术和对用户友好的功能解决潜在的问题,旨在提升您的数字互动体验,使您操作设备的每一刻都更愉悦、更高效。

4. With its unique blend of functionality and style, our product is sure to capture the attention of discerning consumers.
凭借独特的功能和风格,我们的产品一定会吸引有眼光的消费者的注意力。

5. Backed by years of research and development, our product offers cutting-edge technology and unmatched reliability.
经过多年的研发,我们的产品融合了前沿技术,具有无与伦比的可靠性。

6. We are proud to present our latest innovation, a product that embodies our commitment to quality, durability, and user experience.
我们很自豪地展示最新的创新型产品,该产品体现了我们对质量、耐用性和用户体验的承诺。

7. With its cutting-edge features and user-centered design, our product is poised to revolutionize the industry and set new standards for excellence.
凭借领先的功能和以用户为中心的设计,我们的产品将彻底改变行业格局,树立杰出作品的新标准。

8. With over 95% positive customer feedback, our top-loading washing machine stands out for its unique penetrating clean wash system that delivers deep cleaning while protecting clothes from damage.
超过95%的正面客户反馈表明,我们的顶置式洗衣机因其独特的深入清洁洗涤系统而脱颖而出,该系统在深层洁净的同时,能保护衣物不受伤害。

9. Don't let a flat tire ruin your day! Invest in our reliable car inflator and drive with confidence. Contact us now for further details on how to make a purchase.

不要让爆胎毁了你的一天！选择我们的可靠车载打气筒,助您自信驾驶。现在就联系我们,获取购买详情。

10. Experience the future on your wrist with our cutting-edge smartwatch, featuring advanced health tracking and seamless communication. Visit our website now to learn more and take the first step towards a smarter, connected life.

体验手腕上的未来,我们的尖端智能手表具备先进的健康追踪和无缝沟通功能。现在就访问我们的网站,了解更多信息,迈向更智能、更互联的生活。

Task Solving

After studying what has been presented above, you may know how to compose a product introduction successfully.

Consolidation Exercise

1. Please fill in the blanks according to the initial letter.

Nano Coating Agent: The Ultimate Protection for Your Car

(1) B_____ from its nano-coating layer, this product (2) e_____ the gloss and smoothness of car paint, (3) i_____ resistance to acids, alkali, wear, heat, corrosion, and UV rays.

With its (4) u_____ formula, it shields both new and old cars, regardless of color, (5) f_____ acid rain, keeping windshields clear and paintwork vibrant.

Easily (6) a_____ with a soft cloth after spraying, it's suitable for all car surfaces. (7) T_____ by car owners worldwide, it's a must-have for car (8) c_____.

Act now to protect your car with Nano Coating Agent by (9) v_____ our website: www.hzruiming.com to learn more.

(10) S_____ your life with our Nano Coating Agent.

---

2. Please translate the English underlined into Chinese.

---

(1) <u>Venus Electronic Dog: Your Reliable Speed Companion</u>

The Venus Electronic Dog, (2) <u>with its accurate speed detection and timely alarm function</u>, enhances road safety.

It features precise speed measurement, fuel station reminders and red light violation warning, etc. (3) <u>Its real-time speed display without delay ensures safety</u>. Small and adaptable, with a compact body and multiple modes, (4) <u>it's ideal for travelers driving a car with a clear large screen</u>.

> Drivers across the country swear by its effectiveness, making it a must-have for any road trip.
> Don't Risk It. (5) <u>Get the Venus Electronic Dog as your reliable companion</u>.
> Speed accuracy and Zero fine, just at your fingertips.

3. Please translate the Chinese in the brackets into English.

> **Sunshine Brand Solar Energy-Saving Lamp**
>
> _____(欢迎浏览我们的阳光牌太阳能节能灯).
>
> It is a revolution in eco-friendly lighting. _____
> (我们的灯具有无与伦比的节能效率,为您节省电费). Its all-aluminum lightweight design ensures durability and resistance to aging, _____
> (而它的防雨、防锈和高温性能保证使用寿命).
>
> With a wide illumination range, easy installation, and remote control switch, it's the perfect lighting solution.
>
> _____(作为一款畅销品,多年来一直受到成千上万人的欢迎), this lamp is a testament to quality and reliability.
>
> Don't wait; _____(诚邀您用阳光牌太阳能节能灯照亮您的世界) today by visiting our online shop right now!
>
> Light up your life with Sunshine's solar power.

🔑 Writing Practice ////

Directions: David is the design director and general manager of Foremost Sport Co. Ltd. Recently, the company launched a popular street cool casual shoe, and he asked his secretary Mary to write a product introduction for it. The related information of the product is as follows.

> Upper material: mesh
> Sole material: rubber
> Style: Korean version
> Insole material: EVA
> Applicable season: Spring and Autumn
> Product features: fashionable, comfortable, breathable and wear-resistant

Task 5   Recruitment Advertisement

 Learning Objectives

• Learn about the definition, function and types of recruitment advertisement.

• Be familiar with the structure, content and format of recruitment advertisement.

• Master the useful expressions such as words, phrases and sentences for recruitment advertisement.

• Be able to skillfully compose a correct recruitment advertisement in the real business situation.

 Task Situation

With the development of business and the enlargement of scale, Mable's company is planning to look for ten foreign trade salespersons. Mr. Stephen asks Mable to compose a recruitment advertisement according to the following information.

---

1. Responsibilities
-Developing new markets and customers
-Maintaining and managing regular customers
-Publicizing and promoting new products
-Answering customers' questions on products
-Visiting customers and learning about their needs
-Collecting and analyzing sales data
2. Requirements
-Majoring in business English, marketing, e-commerce, etc.
-With a college diploma, a bachelor degree or above preferred
-With work experience in foreign trade preferable
-Fluency in listening, speaking, reading and writing English
-Proficiency in Microsoft Office and social network site such as Youtube and Facebook
-Distinguished management and good communication abilities
-With a flexible thinking, a broad mind and teamwork spirit
-Willing to accept challenges and adopt to travel frequently
This advertisement is valid within one month since it is published.

> Those who are interested in it, please kindly send your resume and a recent digital photo to: hrgzft@yahoo.com.
>
> Add: No.196, Tianhe North Road, Guangzhou, China
>
> Tel: 020-××××××××
>
> Fax: 020-××××××××
>
> Website: www.gzft.com
>
> E-mail: gzft@126.com
>
> Contact: Mr. Alexander, HR Manager

Supposing you are Mabel, how do you finish the task assigned to you?

Questions

- What basic contents are included in a recruitment advertisement?
- How are the structure and format of a recruitment advertisement?
- What points should we pay attention to when composing a recruitment advertisement?

Theory Background

Recruitment advertisement, also known as recruitment ad, is a kind of special advertisement, which is mainly used by an organization or a company to attract or recruit talents to work within it. A good recruitment advertisement can achieve at least two objectives: firstly, it can attract the proper talents to post their resumes; secondly, it can make the company image and core values well known for those interested. Besides, recruitment advertisement may make the first impression of a company for many applicants, so it is very important to take every possible factor into consideration before composing it.

According to its content and function, recruitment advertisement can be classified into as many different kinds as it can be.

Sample Study

Sample 1

Recruitment Advertisement
Job position: Senior Secretary
Brief introduction
Established in 1998, Kings Trading Company is located in the commercial center of South China, Guangzhou. We are a company mainly specializing in producing and exporting

garments. Covering an area of 30,000 square meters, we have a staff of over 2,000 employees. And our products are all exported worldwide.

Responsibilities

- Maintain routine work and office equipment to run smoothly
- Coordinate the relationship with other colleagues and departments
- Schedule appointments for general manager and other division heads
- Translate business documents and reports as required by general manager
- Draft project plans and business proposals as assigned by general manager
- Chase delegated tasks and ensure them to be finished within the deadline
- Supervise the work process to adhere to requirements or progress

Requirements

- Bachelor degree or above, majoring in business administration or related fields
- At least 5 years' experience in joint ventures or multinational corporations
- Excellent oral English and simultaneous Chinese/English translation skills
- Familiar with information management systems and Microsoft Office
- Strong presentation skills as well as interpersonal communication abilities
- Be able to work under pressure and adopt to work overtime frequently

Conditions being offered

We offer an interesting and demanding position with a competitive salary, an attractive year-end bonus, a good opportunity for career development and a pleasant working environment.

Ways of application

Should you be interested, please kindly send your English resume, a recent digital photo and other references to kingshr@yahoo.com or fax to 020-×××× ×××× (Attn: Cathy).

PS: Be sure to highlight the position you apply for in letter subject banner. This advertisement is valid within 20 days after it is published.

Contact way

Add: No.175, Jiefang North Road, Yuexiu District, Guangzhou

Tel: 020-×××× ××××

Fax: 020-×××× ××××

E-mail: kingshr@yahoo.com

Website: www.kings.com

Sample 2

Vacancy for Native English Teacher

FIF English Training Center is seeking three native English teachers. We can offer you with a challenging position, a competitive salary and a top year-end bonus.

Responsibilities:
- Conduct teaching IELTS, TOEFL, GRE, TOEIC, BULATS, etc.
- Develop English training courses and carry out English teaching research
- Compile English teaching materials, handouts, exercises, test papers
- Answer students' questions and enquiry about courses online

Requirements:
- University diploma or above, majoring in English or normal English
- Native English speakers with a TESOL or TEFL Certificate preferable
- English expression fluent and understanding a little Chinese
- Be fond of teaching and willing to communicate with students
- Understanding and respecting different cultures and customs

(We warmly welcome recent graduates to apply for this position.)

You can go to www.fiftrainingcenter.com for further information. Please mail your English resume, diploma, training certificates and expected salary to hrfiftcenter@sina.com within three weeks from today. No personal visit or telephone call without notice.

Add: Room 1608, City Building, Haizhu District, Guangzhou
Tel: 020-×××× ××××
E-mail: hrfiftcenter@sina.com

Sample 3

JOIN OUR PR TEAM—TOP SALARY!

We are a leading PR company and we can offer you a fulfilling and challenging role working with our Director.

You MUST be hard-working, flexible, well-organized and energetic. You will be:
- drawing meeting notices, agenda and preparing for meeting schedules
- compiling meeting documents and testing meeting equipment
- receiving in-coming phone calls and taking telephone messages
- booking tickets and arranging business travel schedules for director
- working as the director's translator or interpreter during his visit abroad

This is a superb opportunity for the right kind of person and we will pay you a top salary as well as a good year-end bonus.

> Call or write today and tell us about yourself.
> Mr. Black, England-European PR, 168B Baker Street, London
> Tel: 0044-20-×××× ××××

Sample 4

> **Are You Ready to Accept Challenges from a Transnational Enterprise?**
>
> Clever Research, with its headquarters in London, is the world's leading online research, trend analysis and news service company in the fashion industry.
>
> With offices all around the world, we are now hiring dynamic candidates to fill the role of Sales Director to cope with our aggressive expansion plans in China.
>
> Reporting to the Regional Sales Director of Asia Pacific, you will be responsible for leading the China sales operation and play a key role in rolling out the brand's accelerated growth strategy in the region. You will develop and deliver the sales strategy and translate it into annual sales plans. Besides, you will work closely with the content team to exchange market intelligence and maximize mutually beneficial content collaboration.
>
> You should have solid experience in delivering sales strategies that demonstrate business acumen and alignment with the company's strategic plan, and managing complexity in a high growth environment. To fit into this challenging role, you will need to have previous experience working in China and experience of starting up a business in China would be an advantage. Experience in an online environment is preferred. You MUST be fluent in English and Mandarin. (Candidates who do not speak Mandarin need NOT apply.)
>
> If you are interested, please kindly send your resume to clever-research @seonline.com or fax to 020-×××× ××××.
>
> This advertisement is valid within 15 days after its being posted.

Sample Structure

> 1. Head/Title
> 2. Job position
> 3. Brief introduction
> 4. Responsibilities
> 5. Requirements
> 6. Conditions
> 7. Ways of application
> 8. Postscript
> 9. Contact way

Structure Analysis

1. Head/Title: To state the subject matter of recruitment advertisement and it usually writes as follows.

Recruitment Advertisement, RECRUITMENT AD
Wanted/ A secretary wanted

---

2. Job position: To state what the job position is.

Job position: Senior Secretary

---

3. Brief introduction: Briefly introduce the history, location, business line, scale of the company and so on, so that the job applicants can have a basic understanding.

Brief introduction:

Established in 1998, Kings Trading Company is located in the commercial center of South China, Guangzhou. We are a company mainly specializing in producing and exporting garments. Covering an area of 30,000 square meters, we have a staff of over 2,000 employees. And our products are all exported worldwide.

---

4. Responsibilities: To describe the job duties that the job applicant should take or carry out.

Responsibilities
- Maintain routine work and office equipment to run smoothly
- Coordinate the relationship with other colleagues and departments
- Schedule appointments for general manager and other division heads
...

---

5. Requirements: To state the qualifications required by the job position such as age, education background, work experience, occupational certificates, language proficiency, computer skills, etc.

Requirements:
- Bachelor degree or above, majoring in business administration or related fields
- At least 5 years' experience in joint ventures or multinational corporations
- Excellent oral English and simultaneous Chinese/English translation skills
...

Module 3 Writing for Publicizing and Advertising

6. Conditions: To state the conditions that can be offered such as salary, bonus, career development, training opportunity, working environment, etc.

> We offer an interesting and demanding position with a competitive salary, an attractive year-end bonus, a good opportunity for career development and a pleasant working environment.

7. Ways of application: To state what documents to be prepared and how and where the documents to be sent.

> Should you be interested, please kindly send your English resume, a recent digital photo and other references to kingshr@yahoo.com or fax to 020-×××× ×××× (Attn: Cathy).

8. Postscript: To state the information to be added and the valid period of the advertisement.

> Be sure to highlight the position you apply for at letter subject banner. This advertisement is valid within 20 days after its being posted.

9. Contact way: To provide the contact means such as person, address, telephone, fax, e-mail, website, etc.

> Add: No.175, Jiefang Road, Yuexiu District, Guangzhou
> Tel: 020-×××× ××××
> Fax: 020-×××× ××××
> E-mail: kingshr@yahoo.com
> Website: www.kings.com

🔑 Writing Tips

1. Use one simple headline, and make the recruitment advertisement headline relevant and clear.

2. Make the advertisement easy to read by using simple language instead of complicated words.

3. Use short sentences so as to keep them clear in meaning and avoid using more than fifteen words in a sentence.

4. Use bullet points and short bite-sized paragraphs to attract more job seekers to read.

5. Try to incorporate something new, innovative, exciting, challenging and so on.

6. Stress your unique selling points, namely try to emphasize what makes our job or company special.

🔑 Useful Expressions

1. Benito, one of the top ranking German industrial groups mainly specializing in mechanical engineering and plant making, is now widening its business in China.

贝尼托是德国名列前茅的工业集团之一,主要从事机械工程、设备制造等业务,现正扩大本公司在华业务。

2. Headquartered in Hong Kong with operations in China's Mainland and abroad, our company is expanding internationally through franchising distributors.

本公司总部设在中国香港,在中国大陆及海外设有分部,通过特许分销商将业务范围扩展到全世界。

3. We are a green environmental cleaning company looking for a manger for our Shanghai Branch.

本公司是一家绿色环保型保洁公司,现正为上海分公司诚聘经理一名。

4. We are now recruiting a proper candidate to fill the role of Sales Director to cope with our aggressive expansion plans in China.

本公司现正寻找合适的人选来承担销售总监一职,以应对我们在华积极扩张的计划。

5. The ideal candidate will have several years' experience of finance management and hold a tertiary accounting qualification.

理想的应聘者须具有数年的财务管理经验,并持有高级会计资格证书。

6. Candidates are supposed to have good communication skills and be able to travel frequently as required.

应聘者应具有良好的交际技能,并能够依照公司安排经常出差。

7. A stable personality and high sense of responsibility are desirable.

应聘者必须具有沉稳的性格和高度的责任感。

8. With enthusiasm and organized working habits are more important than experience.

应聘者要有热情和有条不紊的办事习惯。有无相关经验均可。

9. Work experience in a famous multinational company is preferable.

有在知名跨国公司工作经验者优先录用。

10. With fluent English and Mandarin, Cantonese and Japanese a plus.

要求英语和普通话流利,会粤语及日语者优先录用。

11. A good command of spoken and written English is preferable.

有良好的英文口头和书面表达能力者优先录用。

12. Strong confidence and aggressiveness are a must.

必须有极强的自信心和积极的进取心。

13. Familiar with international trade process will be an added advantage.

熟悉国际贸易流程者尤佳。

14. We will positively improve the quality of employees and supply all kinds of training opportunities for them.

我们将会积极地提升员工的素质,为他们提供各种各样的培训机会。

15. Our company will provide strong growth opportunities for high-caliber and dedicated professionals.

本公司将会为高水平、有奉献精神的专业人才提供富有吸引力的发展机会。

16. We will offer an attractive salary package and good opportunities for career development.

我们将会提供具有吸引力的薪资待遇和良好的职业发展机会。

17. All positions will have highly competitive salaries, medical benefits, year-end bonus, excellent training and career prospects.

所有职位都将获得颇具竞争力的工资、医疗福利、年终奖,以及良好的培训和职业前景。

18. Salary package is negotiable based on individual qualifications.

根据个人资质,工资待遇可协商。

19. Further information, requirements and method of application can be obtained from the recruitment department.

更多详情、应聘条件和申请办法可向招聘部门索取。

20. For eligible candidates, please e-mail your resume with a current photo.

符合条件的应聘者请通过电子邮件发送简历和近照。

21. Should you be interested, please kindly send your updated resume to paul@linkedin.com or fax to 020-×××× ××××.

感兴趣的应聘者可将最新简历发送至 paul@linkedin.com 或传真至 020-×××× ××××。

22. Please kindly send your own handwriting cover letter and resume with a recent photo to the following address.

敬请将亲笔书写的求职信、简历以及近照邮寄到如下地址。

Task Solving

After studying what has been presented above, you may know how to compose a recruitment advertisement successfully.

Consolidation Exercise

1. Please fill in the blanks according to the initial letter.

Guangzhou Evergreen Luggage Co., Ltd.

Join Our Team of Sales Professionals

Guangzhou Evergreen, a famous luggage trade company, has over 320 employees and an annual sales value of 100 million yuan. With the company's business increasingly expanding, we are seeking 20 passionate and dedicated sales professionals.

Requirements:

* (1) B_____ degree or above in the field of marketing, business, trade, etc.

* (2) M_____ 2 years of sales or related work experience

* Proficiency in English and (3) M_____

* Ability to work (4) i_____ and creatively

* Strong communication and negotiation (5) s_____

* (6) W_____ to travel frequently

* Adaptive to work under great (7) p_____

If you are (8) i_____ in joining a fast-paced and dynamic team that is committed to excellence, please send your resume to gzevergreen@sina.com. This advertisement is (9) v_____ within 15 days after its being (10) p_____.

---

2. Please translate the English underlined into Chinese.

International Customer Service (Internship Included)

Responsibilities:

-(1) <u>Answering customers' inquiries and dealing with their orders</u>;

-Timely answering customers' messages and solving their complaints;

-(2) <u>Collecting and sorting out the information of new customers</u>;

-Urging customers to place orders and pay at an appropriate time.

Requirements:

-(3) <u>Integrity, honesty, diligence, patience and team spirit</u>;

-Good communication skills and service attitude;

-(4) Degrees in International Trade, English, French preferred;

-VETS (Vocational English Test System) certificate is preferred.

Contact way:

-Add: Floor 3, Building 1, No. 81, Meiyue Road, China (Shanghai) Pilot Free Trade Zone (China National Machinery Import and Export Corporation Shanghai Pudong Co., Ltd.)

-Tel: 021-××××　××××

-Website: http://www.cmc.com.cn/shanghai

-E-mail: fancier@yahoo.com

-Contact: Mr. Henry

(5) Please kindly send your resume to fancier@yahoo.com.

3. Please translate the Chinese in the brackets into English.

It Is You Who Makes Everything Possible

Guangzhou Pearl River Media Corporation Limited is looking for a Senior Administration Assistant.

Responsibilities:

• _____(根据总部的指示开展各项活动).

• Collect related information and data for the head office.

• Maintain a good relationship with local media and customers.

• _____(在紧急情况下协助应对公共危机).

Requirements:

• With a university degree or above majoring in public relations, journalism, or communication, etc.

• _____(良好的中英文听说能力).

• Be good at communicating with different people.

• _____(有相关工作或实习经验).

• With a flexible mind, quick action, outgoing personality and teamwork spirit.

Valid period:

_____(本广告自发布之日起一个月内有效).

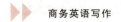

> If you are interested in this position, please kindly send your resume and references to hrgzpm@163.com.
>
> Add: No. 256, Huangshi Road, Baiyun District, Guangzhou
>
> Tel: 020-××××　××××
>
> Fax: 020-××××　××××
>
> E-mail: hrgzpm@163.com

 Writing Practice

Directions: Guangzhou Grace Clothing Company, a leading industry in women's fashion design and manufacturing, is seeking a dynamic HR manager for the president of its New York office. You work as a personnel clerk in the company and your HR director asks you to write a recruitment ad according to the following hints.

> ### 1. Job Description
> -Organize meetings
> -Daily management
> -Respond to urgent requests
> -Coordinate work with other departments
> -Arrange business travels
>
> ### 2. Job Requirements
> -Bachelor's degree or above in secretary or management
>
> -Age between 30 and 35 years old
>
> -At least 8 years' work experience in related fields
>
> -Superior organizational and communicative skills
>
> -Able to work under pressure and adapt to travel frequently
>
> -Initiative, creative and flexible with stable personalities
>
> -Exceptional computer literacy and proficient in oral and written English
>
> This advertisement is valid within one month since its being posted.
>
> Contact person: John Wang
>
> Add: No.186, Tianhe North Road, Guangzhou, China
>
> Tel: 020-××××　××××
>
> E-mail: gzgraceclothing@163.com
>
> Website: www.gzgraceclothing.com

Module 4 Writing for Business Etiquette

Task 1 Invitation Letter

 Learning Objectives

- Learn about the definition, function and types of invitation letter.
- Be familiar with the structure, content and format of invitation letter.
- Master the useful expressions such as words, phrases and sentences for invitation letter.
- Be able to skillfully compose a correct invitation letter in the real business situation.

 Task Situation

In order to strengthen the cooperation, discuss projects and sign a contract with America Fox Trade Company, Mr. Stephen would like to invite Mr. Henry, the purchasing manager, to pay a business visit next month, so he asks Mabel to compose an invitation letter in his name.

Supposing you are Mabel, how do you finish the task assigned to you?

 Questions

- What basic contents are included in an invitation letter?
- How are the structure and format of an invitation letter?
- What points should we pay attention to when composing an invitation letter?

 Theory Background

Invitation letter refers to the letter that is used for inviting customers, business partners, colleagues, relatives, friends, etc. to an important event or occasion such as party, ceremony, anniversary, meeting, fair and product demonstration.

Invitation letter is widely used in business world or personal communication. It can help to improve or reinforce relationships, maintain regular customers, develop potential customers, etc.

According to it function and situation used in, invitation letters can be classified into different types: invitation letter for a meeting/conference/seminar; invitation letter for a party/banquet party/evening party; invitation letter for product presentation or demonstration; invitation letter for a new branch establishment; invitation letter for a company anniversary; invitation letter for an engagement/wedding; invitation letter for the graduation party.

Sample Study

Sample 1: Invitation letter for food exhibition

Shanghai Hongrui Food Company
No.12, Pengjiang Road, Jingan District, Shanghai, China
Tel: 021-××××　××××
Fax: 021-××××　××××
E-mail: hrfsh@126.com

April 18
Tony Ma
Sales Manager
Guangzhou Likefood Food Co., Ltd.
No.36, Beijing Road, Yuexiu District, Guangzhou, China
Tel: 020-××××　××××
Fax: 020-××××　××××
E-mail: likefood@126.com

Dear Mr. Tony Ma,

　　The 30th Shanghai International Food Fair will be open soon, and we are writing to sincerely invite you to attend it.

　　The fair will be held in Shanghai International Exhibition Center from May 8 to 10. Our booth number is CB008, Hall 2, Area B.

　　You are mostly welcome to have a look at our new products.

　　Please let us know your flight details so that we can pick you up at the airport.

　　We would be very appreciated if you could give us a reply not later than April 28. We are looking forward to meeting you at the fair.

Yours truly,
Grace Lin
Market Manager
Shanghai Hongrui Food Company
No. 12, Pengjiang Road, Jingan District, Shanghai
Tel: 021-××××　××××
Fax: 021-××××　××××
E-mail: hrfsh@126.com

Enclosure: Application form

Sample 2: Invitation letter for completion ceremony

South China Mechanics Equipment Company
No.1068, Huangpu Avenue, Huangpu District, Guangzhou, China
Tel: 020-××××　××××; Fax: 020-××××　××××
E-mail: scmehuangpu@yahoo.com
August 11

Dear Mr. Harrison,

　　In order to celebrate the completion of our new factory, we sincerely invite you to the ceremony which will be held at 8:48 a.m. on September 10.

　　It is an important milestone for our company, and it is also the result of our customers' support at home and overseas, so we are hoping that you can be present witnessing the significant occasion together with us.

　　We would be thankful if you could inform us of your arrival time in advance, and we are waiting for your early answer.

Yours faithfully,
Charlie Chen
Chief of Executive

Sample 3: Invitation letter for giving a lecture

March 1
Dear Prof. Higgins,

　　We will hold a series of activities on our campus culture. Therefore, we are writing to sincerely invite you to be present. The activity will be held from March 30 to 31. We would like you to visit our campus and give us a lecture on "How to Construct Campus Culture". Besides, we hope that you can put forward some suggestions on our campus culture.

　　Please tell us your flight details so that we can arrange to pick you up at the airport.

　　We shall be much obliged if you could answer us as early as possible at your convenience. We are looking forward to your presence.

Yours sincerely,
Li Ming
President
Guangzhou University

Sample 4: Invitation letter for attending a party

January 9

Dear Mr. Green,

  We are planning a party celebrating the 24th anniversary of our company. We would like to extend an invitation to you to attend the party.

  The party will be at the Hilton Hotel, Detroit, beginning at 9.30 a.m. on Wednesday, January 15, and dress will be formal business wear.

  We hope that you will be able to join us to celebrate this remarkable occasion. We look forward to seeing you on Wednesday, January 15.

Yours sincerely,
Robert Miles
Chief Executive Officer

Sample Structure

1. Letterhead (if necessary)
2. Date
3. Inside name and address (if necessary)
4. Salutation
5. Body (opening, middle, closing)
6. Complimentary close
7. Signature
8. Job title (if necessary)
9. Company, organization (if necessary)
10. Contact way (if necessary)
11. Enclosures (if necessary)

Structure Analysis

1. Letterhead: To show the writer's address, usually located in the right top corner.

Shanghai Hongrui Food Company,
No.12, Pengjiang Road, Jingan District, Shanghai
Tel: 021-×××× ××××
Fax: 021-×××× ××××
E-mail: hrfsh@126.com

2. Date: To state when the letter is written, placed in the left top corner and just below the letterhead.

```
April 18
```

3. Inside name and address: To show the receiver's name and address, located in the left top corner and just above the salutation.

```
Tony Ma
Sales Manager
Guangzhou Likefood Food Co., Ltd.
No.36, Beijing Road, Yuexiu District, Guangzhou, China
Tel: 020-×××× ××××
Fax: 020-×××× ××××
E-mail: likefood@126.com
```

4. Salutation: To show respect to the receiver, often laid in the top left corner and just below the inside name and address.

```
Dear Mr. Tony Ma
```

5. Body: To state the main content that the letter is concerned about; it is the most important part and includes opening, middle and closing.

```
    The 30th Shanghai International Food Fair will be open soon, and we are writing to sincerely invite you to attend it.
    The fair will be held in Shanghai International Exhibition Center from May 8 to 10. Our booth number is CB008, Hall 2, Area B.
    You are mostly welcome to have a look at our new products.
    ...
```

6. Complimentary close: To show the writer's courtesy, set in the bottom and just above the signature.

```
Yours sincerely
Truly yours
```

7. Signature: To show by whom the writer is written; for the purpose of politeness, signature written in hand is preferred.

```
Grace Lin
```

8. Job title: To show what position the writer holds.

Market Manager

9. Company, organization: To show where the writer works.

Shanghai Hongrui Food Company

10. Contact way: To provide information about the writer's contact means such as address, telephone, fax, e-mail, website, etc.

No. 12, Pengjiang Road, Jingan District, Shanghai   Tel: 021-××××　××××   Fax: 021-××××　××××   E-mail: hrfsh@126.com

11. Enclosure: To attach some documents or materials concerned but not convenient to state in the body part.

Enclosure: Application form

Body Structure

The body usually consists of the following three parts.

1. Opening   2. Middle   3. Closing

Body Analysis

1. Opening: To state the reasons for invitation as well as the purpose for writing.

The 30th Shanghai International Food Fair will be open soon, and we are writing to sincerely invite you to attend it.

2. Middle: To provide the detailed information about the event or activity such as time, date, place, participants and so on.

The fair will be held in Shanghai International Exhibition Center from May 8 to 10. Our booth number is CB008, Hall 2, Area B.   You are mostly welcome to have a look at our new products.   ...

3. Closing: To express your thanks as well as your wishes or expectations.

> We would be very appreciated if you could give us a reply not later than April 28. We are looking forward to meeting you at the fair.

Writing Tips

1. In general, try to write it short, sincerely and appropriately.
2. In the opening, state your reason for invitation and your purpose for writing.
3. In the middle, outline the key information such as time, date, place and so on.
4. In the closing, be sure to show your expectations or best wishes.
5. State the deadline for the invitees to confirm accepting or declining.
6. Be sure to mention any specifications about dress code if necessary.
7. Try to send your invitation letter two weeks or more in advance.
8. Make sure there is no punctuation, grammatical or spelling errors before sending it.

Useful Expressions

1. I am writing on behalf of general manager to invite you to give all staff of our company a lecture on marketing strategies.
现谨代表总经理去函：邀请您为本公司全体员工就销售策略做讲座。

2. We are writing to sincerely invite you to attend the Canton Fair to be held in October this year.
兹去函，诚邀您参加今年10月举行的广交会。

3. The Food Fair will be held in Shanghai International Exhibition Center from May 8 to 10.
食品展将于5月8日至10日在上海国际展览中心举行。

4. We sincerely hope that you and Susan will take part in the dancing party this evening.
我们衷心地希望您和苏珊能参加今晚的舞会。

5. In order to celebrate this significant occasion, we are inviting you to be present at the opening ceremony.
为庆祝这一重要时刻，现邀请您出席开幕仪式。

6. It is my pleasure (a great honor for me) to invite you to the summit for senior managers.
本人非常高兴（荣幸）地邀请您出席高级经理人峰会。

7. We kindly invite you to attend the International Fair which will be held at Dalian Xinghai Convention and Exhibition Center from May 6 to 10.

我们诚挚地邀请您参加5月6日到10日在大连星海会展中心举行的国际博览会。

8. It is our pleasure to invite you to the banquet that will be held in Rose Hall of Garden Hotel on July 5.

我们很高兴地邀请您参加7月5日在花园酒店玫瑰厅举行的宴会。

9. Please kindly tell us your flight details so that we could pick you up at the airport.

请告知航班详情,以便我们前往机场接您。

10. To commemorate this special occasion, we will host a dinner party on the evening of March 12.

为纪念这一特殊时刻,我们将于3月12日晚上举行宴会。

11. All costs incurred will be borne by our company.

所发生的一切费用均由本公司承担。

12. Please advise us of your arrival time if you are able to attend.

如能参加,请通知我们到达时间。

13. Your presence at the opening ceremony will be much appreciated.

如果您能出席开幕式,我们将不胜感激。

14. Will you send your RSVP card to the secretariat no later than December 18?

请您于12月18日前将回执寄至秘书处。

15. It would be a great honor to us if you would accept our invitation.

如果您能接受邀请,我们将不胜荣幸。

16. We would be very appreciated if you could give us a reply not later than April 8.

如果您能在4月8日前给予回复,我们将不胜感激。

17. We would feel honored if you could come to the meeting.

如果您能参加会议,我们将不胜荣幸。

18. We should be very grateful if you could honor us with your presence.

如果您能赏脸光临,我们将不胜感激。

19. We are looking forward to your presence.

我们期待您的莅临。

20. We are anticipating your early confirming.

我们期待着您尽快确认。

 Task Solving

After studying what has been presented above, you may know how to compose an invitation letter successfully.

Consolidation Exercise

1. Please fill in the blanks according to the initial letter.

Dear Global Partner,

  I am writing to invite you to attend the (1) u_____ Canton Fair in 2024, where Wanner Corporation will be (2) s_____ its latest products. The Canton Fair is one of the largest trade events in the world, (3) a_____ thousands of global businesses and buyers.

  As a leading cosmetics (4) m_____, we believe that our new products will not only (5) m_____ the evolving needs of consumers, but also provide unique value for our partners.

  During the Canton Fair, we will host several activities (6) d_____ to foster meaningful discussions and collaborations. We encourage you to take (7) a_____ of this opportunity to learn more about our products, (8) e_____ potential partners, and discuss future business ventures.

  Your (9) p_____ at the Canton Fair would be a significant addition to our event. Your expertise and knowledge would greatly (10) c_____ to the success of our exhibition.

  We look forward to your attendance, and please let us know if you have any questions.

  Best regards!

Wanner Corporation

2. Please translate the English underlined into Chinese.

January 12

Dear Mr. Karl,

  I am writing as the secretary of the organizing committee for the 3rd Global New Energy Vehicle Hybrid Power Conference and Autonomous Driving Innovation Summit, which will take place in Shanghai on March 30th and 31st.

  (1) <u>We would like to sincerely invite you to attend this prestigious event</u> and give a speech on the topic of "Hybrid Power Development". As the Technical Director of T&G Platform and the Chief Engineer of the Engine System, (2) <u>your expertise and insights in this field are sure to be highly sought after</u>.

  We would like to emphasize that (3) <u>all expenses related to your accommodation and meals during the conference</u> will be fully covered by the organizing committee. (4) <u>Please let us know as soon as possible if you are available to the conference</u>.

(5) <u>Attending this conference will provide you with an excellent opportunity</u> to network with industry experts, share knowledge, and learn about the latest trends and developments in the field of new energy vehicles and autonomous driving.

We look forward to hearing from you soon, and we hope that you can attend our conference. Thank you for your time and consideration.

Best regards!

Mary
Secretary of Conference Committee

3. Please translate the Chinese in the brackets into English.

Dear Professor Tony Wang,

_____ (第15届世界数字经济论坛将于下个月举行). We are writing to _____ _____ (诚挚地邀请您做一场关于数字经济的报告).

It is well known that you are a very famous expert in the digital economy. And _____ _____ (希望您能与我们分享有关该领域的独到见解).

Please _____ (在6月25日前把报告通过电子邮件发给会议组委会), so that we can make careful arrangements in advance. _____ (如能早日回复，我们将不胜感激), and we are looking forward to seeing you soon in London in the near future.

Faithfully yours,
Ms. Cathy Li

Writing Practice

Direction: Supposing you are Jane, secretary of Fair-lady Clothing Co., Ltd. Your company is going to hold a new product demonstration fair at Guangzhou Exhibition Center on March 5. Miss Cherry, your general manager, would like to invite Mr. Hunter, the Sales Manager of Paris Evergreen Clothes Company, to attend the fair. She asks you to write an invitation letter in her name.

Task 2 Acceptance Letter

 Learning Objectives

- Learn about the definition, function and types of acceptance letter.
- Be familiar with the structure, content and format of acceptance letter.
- Master the useful expressions such as words, phrases and sentences for acceptance letter.
- Be able to skillfully compose a correct acceptance letter in the real business situation.

 Task Situation

Yesterday (July 17) Mr. Stephen received a letter from America Fox Trade Company, in which Mr. Henry, the purchasing manager, invites him to pay a business return visit next month. Mr. Stephen would like to accept the invitation, so he asks Mabel to compose an acceptance letter on behalf of him.

Supposing you are Mabel, how do you finish the task assigned to you?

 Questions

- What basic contents are included in an acceptance letter?
- How are the structure and format of an acceptance letter?
- What points should we pay attention to when composing an acceptance letter?

 Theory Background

Acceptance letter refers to the letter written to accept someone's invitation. Usually an invitation must be promptly acknowledged. Therefore, if an invitation is accepted, it is advisable to write back to the inviter promptly so that some preparations can be made in advance such as booking meeting rooms, hotels, tickets, etc.

According to its content and function, acceptance letter can be classified into as many kinds as it can be.

Sample Study

Sample 1: Acceptance letter for food fair

Guangzhou Likefood Food Co., Ltd.
No.36, Beijing Road, Yuexiu District, Guangzhou
Tel: 020-×××× ××××
Fax: 020-×××× ××××
E-mail: likefood@126.com

April 19
Grace Lin
Market Manager
Shanghai Hongrui Food Company
Tel: 021-×××× ××××
Fax: 021-×××× ××××
E-mail: hrfsh@126.com
No.12, Pengjiang Road, Jingan District, Shanghai

Dear Miss Grace,

  Thank you for your kind invitation of March 18. I am writing to tell you that I take pleasure in accepting your invitation and will be present at the food fair to be held from May 8 to 10.

  My flight number is SA 6688, arriving at Shanghai Hongqiao International Airport at 18:00 on May 7, and we will stay in Ritz-Carlton Hotel. There are four people in our delegation.

  Thank you for your kind invitation again. I am anticipating having a good look at your new products and wish the fair will be a great success.

Yours truly,
Tony Ma
Sales Manager
Guangzhou Likefood Food Co., Ltd.

Sample 2: Acceptance letter for completion ceremony

August 12

Dear Mr. Chen,

  Thank you for your letter dated August 11, in which you invite me to attend the completion ceremony of your new factory. I am glad to tell you that I will accept your sincere invitation.

  I will be arriving at Guangzhou Baiyun International Airport at 17:30 on September 9, taking a flight of MU 9986. I feel really happy that your company has been ever-expanding and made so many achievements in the past several years.

  Thank you very much for your sincere invitation again, and I hope to see you very soon and witness the significant occasion together with you.

Yours faithfully,

Mr. Harrison

Chief of Executive

Sample 3: Acceptance letter for giving a lecture

March 2

Dear President Li Ming,

  Thank you for your letter of March 1 inviting me to attend the series activities of your college's campus culture. I am very pleased to accept your kind invitation.

  I will give a lecture entitled "How to Construct Campus Culture". And I will put forward some advice on the campus culture. Then I would like to visit your campus.

  Our flight number is AE 5688 and we will arrive at the Baiyun International Airport at 17:30 on March 29. There are three people accompanying with me.

  I am looking forward to visiting your college.

Yours sincerely,

Higgins

Professor

Yale University

Sample 4: Acceptance letter for attending a party

January 10

Dear Mr. Miles,

  I have received your letter of January 9 with thanks. I am very pleased to accept your kind invitation to the party celebrating the 24th anniversary of your company.

I feel very honored to have such a precious opportunity to attend the party. I will be attending the party on time.

Please accept my hearty congratulations on this remarkable occasion. We are very pleased that you have achieved such great success in your sales during the past decades.

Thank you very much for your sincere invitation again, and I am looking forward to seeing you in Detroit next Wednesday.

Yours sincerely,
Richard Harris
Managing Director

Sample Structure

1. Head (if necessary)
2. Date
3. Inside name and address (if necessary)
4. Salutation
5. Body
6. Complimentary close
7. Signature
8. Job title (if necessary)
9. Company, organization, institution (if necessary)
10. Contact way (if necessary)
11. Enclosures (if necessary)

Body Structure

The body usually consists of the following three parts.

1. Opening
2. Middle
3. Closing

Body Analysis

1. Opening: To express your thanks for invitation and state your purpose for writing.

Thank you for your kind invitation of March 18. I am writing to tell you that I take pleasure in accepting your invitation and will be present at the food fair to be held from May 8 to 10.

2. Middle: To provide the detailed information such as arriving time, stay place and participants.

My flight number is SA 6688, arriving at Shanghai Hongqiao International Airport at 18:00 on May 7, and we will stay in Ritz-Carlton Hotel. There are four people in our delegation.

3. Closing: To express your thanks again as well as your wishes or expectations.

Thank you for your kind invitation again. I am anticipating having a look at your new products and wish the fair will be a great success.

 Writing Tips

1. In general, try to write it short, sincerely and appropriately.
2. In the opening, express your thanks for the invitation and state your purpose for writing.
3. Restate the date, address, and time of the event. It may prevent the possible misunderstandings.
4. In the middle, provide the detailed information such as arriving time, flight number, participants and so on.
5. In the closing, express your thanks again as well as wishes or expectations.
6. Make sure there is no punctuation, grammatical or spelling errors before sending it.
7. An acceptance letter must be a definite. An open ended or ambiguous acceptance is not satisfactory.
8. Try to send your acceptance letter as soon as possible.

 Useful Expressions

1. We have received your letter of invitation dated August 22 with thanks.
我们已收到贵方8月22日发出的邀请函,对此非常感激。
2. Many thanks for your letter of invitation sent on July 18, sincerely inviting me to the dinner party to be held on July 25.
非常感谢贵方7月18日发来的邀请函,诚挚地邀请我参加7月25日举行的晚宴。
3. Thank you very much for the invitation letter of March 18, in which you warmly invite

us to the food fair.

非常感谢您3月18日的邀请函,热情地邀请我们参加食品展览会。

4.We are very delighted to tell you that we will accept your invitation to the academic lecture.

很高兴地告知您,我们将会接受贵方的邀请参加学术报告会。

5.I am writing to tell you that I take pleasure in accepting the invitation and will be present at the seminar on finance management.

兹去函,告知贵方:我很乐意接受您们的邀请,出席有关财务管理的研讨会。

6.I am very pleased to receive your sincere invitation to the opening ceremony of your company to be held on July 23.

我很荣幸收到您的诚挚邀请,邀请我参加贵公司7月23日举行的开业典礼。

7.I am very happy to accept your kind invitation to the cocktail party to be held in Hilton Hotel at 7:00 p.m. on December 2.

我很高兴接受您的邀请,参加12月2日晚上7点在希尔顿酒店举行的鸡尾酒会。

8.In reply to your kind invitation of May 10, we will participate in the evening party celebrating the 25th anniversary of your company.

兹回复贵公司5月10日的诚挚邀请,届时我们会参加贵公司的25周年庆祝晚会。

9.We have decided to attend the meeting to be held from September 5 to 8.

我们已决定参加9月5日至8日举行的会议。

10.Enclosed please find a copy of application form for conference.

随函附会议申请表一份,请查收。

11.We are awaiting to have a good look at your new products.

我们期待着能够仔细欣赏贵公司的新产品。

12.We wish the exhibition will be a great success.

祝愿此次展会取得圆满成功。

13.I'm looking forward to becoming personally acquainted with you next week.

我期待下周能够亲自见到您。

14.Thank you very much for your kind invitation again, and we are anticipating to see you at the fair with keen desire.

再次感谢您的热情邀请,我们热切期待在展览会上见到您。

Task Solving

After studying what has been presented above, you may know how to compose an acceptance letter successfully.

Consolidation Exercise

1. Please fill in the blanks according to the initial letter.

Dear Wanner Corporation,

I am (1) p_____ to receive your invitation to the Canton Fair in 2024, where I look forward to exploring your latest products. As a global partner, I am always interested in (2) s_____ up-to-date with the latest trends and technologies in the (3) i_____.

I am confident that your new products will encounter warm (4) w_____ by consumers. The Canton Fair is an excellent (5) p_____ for fostering business relationships and discovering new market trends, and I am (6) e_____ to be part of this event. I appreciate the (7) e_____ you have give in planning the event. I will make every (8) a_____ to attend the Canton Fair and take advantage of the opportunities it will offer.

Thank you for your kind invitation and (9) h_____. I am looking forward to a successful Canton Fair experience and the opportunity to work (10) c_____ with Wanner Corporation in the future.

Sincerely yours,
Mr. Martin
T&D Cardiff Company

2. Please translate the English underlined into Chinese.

January 13
Dear Miss Mary,

Thank you very much for your invitation. (1) <u>I will be present at the meeting on time</u> and deliver a speech on the theme of "Hybrid Power Development".

(2) <u>I am very interested in the theme and topics</u> of this meeting, so I will do my best to prepare for it. And (3) <u>I will be glad to share valuable insights with others</u> at the meeting.

Regarding the cost of accommodation and meals, (4) <u>I am very grateful for the generous support</u> of the organizing committee. I will arrange the relevant matters properly.

(5) <u>Thank you again for your invitation and support</u>. We look forward to meeting and communicating with you and other experts at the meeting.

Sincerely yours,
Jackson Lu

3. Please translate the Chinese in the brackets into English.

Dear Miss Linda,

  _____(贵方7月24日的来信已收到,感谢), in which you invite me to the 26th International Textile Fair to be held in Shanghai on August 15. I am writing to tell you that _____ (我很乐意接受贵方诚挚的邀请).

  I am interested in your products and I will have a good look at them on that day. _____ (我将乘坐EU3388号航班抵达上海) at 14:00 p.m. on July 22. _____ (再次感谢您热情的邀请) and the effort you have made for the successful commencement of this fair. _____ (衷心祝愿此次展会取得巨大成功). I am eager to see you in Shanghai very soon.

Faithfully yours,
Tony Wang

Writing Practice

  Directions: Today (February 26) Mr. Hunter, the sales manager of Paris Evergreen Clothes Company, receives a letter from Miss Cherry, general manager of Fair-lady Clothing Co., Ltd., in which Miss Cherry invites him to attend her company's new product demonstration fair. The fair will be held at Guangzhou Exhibition Center at 9:00 a.m. on March 8. Mr. Hunter would like to accept the invitation, so he asks Nancy, his secretary, to write an acceptance letter to Miss Cherry in his name. The details are as follows.

1. Flight number: MU 5563
2. Arriving time and date: 17:30 p.m. on March 7
3. The number of delegation: 6
4. Other information if necessary

Task 3　Refusal Letter

 Learning Objectives

- Learn about the definition, function and types of refusal letter.
- Be familiar with the structure, content and format of refusal letter.
- Master the useful expressions such as words, phrases and sentences for refusal letter.
- Be able to skillfully compose a correct refusal letter in the real business situation.

 Task Situation

Yesterday (July 17) Mr. Stephen received a letter from America Fox Trade Company, in which Mr. Henry, the purchasing manager, invites him to pay a business return visit next month. However, owing to a previous engagement, Mr. Stephen is unable to accept the invitation, so he asks Mabel to compose a refusal letter on behalf of him.

Supposing you are Mabel, how do you finish the task assigned to you?

 Questions

- What basic contents are included in a refusal letter?
- How are the structure and format of a refusal letter?
- What points should we pay attention to when composing a refusal letter?

 Theory Background

The refusal letter refers to the letter written to decline someone's invitation owing to some reasons. As usual, if an invitation is refused, it is preferable to respond back promptly so that the host can make some adjustments or prepare other alternatives accordingly. Refusal letter must be definite, and any open-end or ambiguous expressions are not advisable.

According to its function, refusal letter can be classified into as many kinds as it can be.

Sample Study

Sample 1: Refusal letter for food fair

Guangzhou Likefood Food Co., Ltd.
No. 36, Beijing Road, Yuexiu District, Guangzhou
Tel: 020-××××　××××
Fax: 020-××××　××××
E-mail:likefood@126.com

April 19
Grace Lin
Market Manager
Shanghai Hongrui Food Company
Tel: 021-××××　××××
Fax: 021-××××　××××
E-mail: hrfsh@126.com
No. 12, Pengjiang Road, Jingan District, Shanghai

Dear Miss Grace,

  Thank you for your letter dated April 18, inviting me to the food fair that will be held in Shanghai International Exhibition Center from May 8 to 10. However, I am regretful to tell you that I will be unable to accept your sincere invitation.

  I have been scheduled in advance and will have to attend a food material fair in Germany during that time. I feel so sorry that there is a time conflict for the two fairs and I am unable to make both, hoping you can understand the reasons that prevent my attendance and accept my genuine apologies. I am very interested in the latest development in food industry. If there is another fair relating to this field next time, please kindly inform me and I will try my best to attend it.

  Thank you for your kind invitation again. I sincerely wish this fair will be accomplished successfully.

Yours truly,
Tony Ma
Sales Manager
Guangzhou Likefood Food Co., Ltd.
No. 36, Beijing Road, Yuexiu District, Guangzhou
Tel: 020-××××　××××
Fax: 020-××××　××××
E-mail: likefood@126.com

Sample 2: Refusal letter for completion ceremony

August 12

Dear Mr. Chen,

  Thank you for your cordial invitation of August 11, in which you invite me to the completion ceremony of your new factory. But I am regretful to tell you that I cannot attend it.

  Owing to a previous engagement, I will attend the 21st World Mechanics Equipment Exhibition to be held in Paris from September 9 to 12. Please accept my true apology for not being able to attend the ceremony and witness the significant occasion together with you.

  Many thanks for your warm invitation again. I sincerely hope this ceremony will be a complete success and look forward to visiting you in the near future.

Yours faithfully,

Mr. Harrison

Chief of Executive

Sample 3: Refusal letter for giving a lecture

March 2

Dear President Li Ming,

  Thank you for your letter of March 1 inviting me to attend the series activities of your college's campus culture. Unfortunately, I am unable to accept your kind invitation due to a previous engagement.

  How I would like to attend your series activities! But I will go to France to participate in an academic forum on that day. I hope there will be another opportunity to visit your college in the near future.

  Once again I would express my sincere apology for that. I wish it will be a great success. I am looking forward to seeing you soon.

Yours sincerely,

Higgins

Professor

Yale University

Sample 4: Refusal letter for attending a party

January 10

Dear Mr. Stevens,

  Thank you very much for your kind invitation to the party celebrating the 24th anniversary of your company. Please accept my hearty congratulations on this remarkable occasion. We are very pleased that you have achieved such great success in your sales during the past decades.

  Unfortunately, my schedule in January will not allow me to attend this significant celebration. Urgent matters that cannot be rescheduled make it necessary for me to be in Berlin at that time. I certainly hope you understand the reasons preventing my attendance.

  Thank you for your sincere invitation again. I'm looking forward to the long-term smooth and close cooperation between our two corporations.

Yours sincerely,
Richard Harris
Managing Director

Sample Structure

1. Letterhead (if necessary)
2. Date
3. Inside name and address (if necessary)
4. Salutation
5. Body (opening, middle, closing)
6. Complimentary close
7. Signature
8. Job title (if necessary)
9. Company, organization (if necessary)
10. Contact way (if necessary)
11. Enclosures (if necessary)

Body Structure

The body usually consists of the following three parts.

1. Opening
2. Middle
3. Closing

Body Analysis

1. Opening: To express your thanks and state the purpose for writing.

> Thank you for your letter dated April 18, inviting me to the food fair that will be held in Shanghai International Exhibition Center from May 8 to 10. However, I am regretful to tell you that I will be unable to accept your sincere invitation.

2. Middle: To state the reasons for refusing the invitation.

> I have been scheduled in advance and will have to attend a food material fair in Germany during that time. I feel so sorry that there is a time conflict for the two fairs and I am unable to make both...

3. Closing: To express your thanks again as well as wishes or expectations.

> Thank you for your kind invitation again. I sincerely wish this fair will be accomplished successfully.

Writing Tips

1. Express your sincere thanks for the invitation.
2. Clearly express you are unable to accept the invitation.
3. State the reasons for declining the invitation.
4. Express your thanks again and best wishes.
5. Sometimes you can make another appointment or schedule for next time.
6. The refusal letter should be courteous and must be promptly answered.
7. Refusal letter must be clear and any open-ended or ambiguous reply is not preferable.

Useful Expressions

1. Many thanks for your letter inviting me to be a keynote speaker at the 10th International New Energy Automobile Forum.
非常感谢贵方来函,邀请我在第十届国际新能源汽车论坛做主旨发言人。

2. I feel very honored to receive your cordial invitation, but much to my regret I can not attend the meeting to be held on July 26.
收到贵方诚挚的邀请,我深感荣幸。但很遗憾,我无法参加7月26日举行的会议。

3. Your invitation to the sales meeting dated May 15 has been received with thanks, but unfortunately I will be unable to attend it.

本人已收到贵公司于5月15日发出的销售会议邀请,对此非常感谢。但很遗憾,本人无法参加。

4. I appreciate very much your letter of yesterday, in which you invite me to attend the product demonstration your company will hold on March 3.

非常感谢您昨日来函,邀请我参加3月3日举行的产品发布会。

5. I am sorry that I have another engagement on that day, so I can not attend the year-end summary meeting of March 8.

很遗憾,因那一天另有约定,我不能参加3月8日举行年度总结大会。

6. Please accept my sincere regret for not being able to take part in the business evening banquet to be held on November 16.

本人不能参加11月16日的商务晚宴,请接受本人诚挚的歉意。

7. Owning to a previous appointment, I regret that I cannot accept your cordial invitation to luncheon.

很遗憾,因有约在先,本人不能接受您诚挚的午宴邀请。

8. I feel very regretful that a previous schedule prevents me from accepting your kind invitation to the 21st World Fortune Forum.

很遗憾,因先前已有安排,我不能接受您的盛情邀请,无法参加第21届世界财富论坛。

9. Unfortunately, I have been busy these days, and I can't attend the New Year's Evening Party.

很遗憾,本人最近较忙,故无法参加新年晚会。

10. Unfortunately, I could not accept your invitation due to a previous arrangement to attend an academic seminar.

很遗憾,因之前已安排参加一场学术研讨会,故我无法接受您的邀请。

11. How I wish I could be present at the fair! But I have been scheduled in advance to be attending a food material fair in Singapore during that time.

我多么希望能参加此次展览会!但我事先已有安排,届时将参加在新加坡举行的食品材料展。

12. Most unfortunately, we shall be unable to accept your kind invitation on account of a previous engagement.

非常抱歉,由于有约在先,我们无法接受您的盛情邀请。

13. Please accept my true apology for not being able to attend the 15th anniversary ceremony of your company at 9:00 a.m. on October 10.

本人无法参加贵公司10月10日上午9点举行的15年周年庆祝仪式,请接受本人诚挚的歉意。

14. Unfortunately, I shall be on business on December 7 and will not, therefore, be able to attend the banquet you are holding.

遗憾的是,我12月7日要出差,因此不能参加您们举行的宴会。

15. Much to my regret, I will participate in an opening ceremony on that day and cannot attend the sales meeting to be held by your company.

十分遗憾,那天我要参加开幕仪式,故无法出席贵公司召开的销售会议。

16. I feel so sorry that the time for the two parties is conflicting and I cannot make both, so I shall not be able to take part in your dinner party.

非常抱歉,两次宴会的时间相互冲突,本人又无法两者兼顾,所以不能参加您们的宴会。

17. I hope you can understand the reasons preventing my attendance and accept my earnest apologies.

希望您理解我无法参加的原因,并接受我诚挚的歉意。

18. If there is another conference relating to this field held by your university next time, please inform me in advance.

如贵校将来再次举行与此领域有关的会议,请提前通知我。

19. Thank you for your kind invitation again and I sincerely wish this fair will be accomplished successfully.

再次感谢您诚挚的邀请,衷心祝愿展会取得圆满成功。

20. I sincerely hope the meeting will be a complete success and look forward to visiting your company in the near future.

衷心祝愿此次会议取得圆满成功,我期待在不久的将来拜访贵公司。

21. I cordially wish the forum will be completed successfully and anticipate to see you in the near future.

衷心祝愿此次论坛取得圆满成功,期待在不久的将来见到您。

22. I am looking forward to attending the exhibition next time, and I sincerely hope the event will be successful.

期待下次能参加贵公司的展会,衷心祝愿此次展会取得成功。

Task Solving

After studying what has been presented above, you may know how to compose a refusal letter successfully.

Consolidation Exercise

1. Please fill in the blanks according to the initial letter.

Dear Wanner Corporation,

  I am (1) t_____ for your invitation to the Canton Fair in 2024, where I wish to have a good look at your latest products. (2) H_____ I regret to inform you that I will not be able to attend the event.

I am fully (3) a_____ of the value of the Canton Fair as an excellent platform for discovering new business opportunity, and I (4) d_____ to take part in this event, but (5) m_____ to my regret, I have to attend another fair to be (6) h_____ in Sydney at that time. I feel very sorry for that and please (7) a_____ my apologies.

I am very interested in you new products, and I hope you can (8) s_____ me some product catalogue after the fair. If there is another (9) r_____ fair next time, please inform me in advance. I will try my best to attend.

Thank you once again for inviting me to the fair. I am looking forward to (10) m_____ you in the near future.

Sincerely yours,
Mr. Martin
T&D Cardiff Company

2. Please translate the English underlined into Chinese.

May 15

Dear Mr. David,

Thank you for your letter of May 14, (1) <u>in which you invite me to attend the summit forum</u> on mobile phone design, research and development, and production to be held in New Delhi on October 20. I am honored to receive your invitation, but I regret to inform you that (2) <u>I will be unable to participate in this event</u>.

(3) <u>I am sorry that I have another engagement that day</u> and I will participate in our Clever Company's Clever 18 mobile phone new product launch. (4) <u>I hope you can understand my difficulties</u>. If there is another forum next time, please kindly tell me in advance.

Thank you again for inviting me and (5) <u>we cordially wish the forum will be a great success</u>.

Sincerely yours,
Lei Jun
Clever Technology Co., Ltd.

3. Please translate the Chinese in the brackets into English.

Dear Prof. Smith,

　　Thank you for your letter of March 18 _____
（邀请我做主旨演讲）on the latest development of smart mobile phone at the World Communication Technology Forum _____（4月12日在深圳举行）.

I feel deeply honored, _____ (但很遗憾,我事先有约), I cannot attend the forum during that time. _____
_____ (请接受我诚挚的歉意).

Besides, I am very interested in the lasted development in communication technology, if there is other conference relating to the field in the future, I would make best balance to make the schedule.

At last, _____ (祝愿论坛取得圆满成功). I am looking forward to seeing you in the near future.

Yours sincerely,
Thomas Song

Writing Practice

Directions: Today (February 26) Mr. Hunter, the sales manager of Paris Evergreen Clothes Company, receives a letter from Miss Cherry, general manager of Fair-lady Clothing Co., Ltd., in which Miss Cherry invites him to attend her company's new product demonstration fair. The fair will be held at Guangzhou Exhibition Center at 9:00 a.m. on March 8. However, Mr. Hunter will be in New York on that day attending an important conference and cannot attend the fair, so he asks Nancy, his secretary, to write a declining letter to Miss Cherry in his name.

Task 4　Thank-you Letter

Learning Objectives

- Learn about the definition, function and types of thank-you letter.
- Be familiar with the structure, content and format of thank-you letter.
- Master the useful expressions such as words, phrases and sentences for thank-you letter.
- Be able to skillfully compose a correct thank-you letter in the real business situation.

Task Situation

Last week, Mr. Stephen paid a return business visit to Mr. Henry's company. During the entire trip, Mr. Stephen got a warm reception. To express his appreciation for Mr. Henry's hospitality, Mr. Stephen asks Mabel to compose a thank-you letter to Mr. Henry in his name.

Supposing you are Mabel, how do you finish the task assigned to you?

Questions

- What basic contents are included in a thank-you letter?
- How are the structure and format of a thank-you letter?
- What points should we pay attention to when composing a thank-you letter?

Theory Background

A thank-you letter is a letter written to express one's thanks for other's hospitality, presents, support, invitations, contributions, etc. A thank-you letter is frequently employed in social interaction and business communication between people or companies. It can promote business relations and increase interpersonal feelings. Even when one has thanked someone in person, a written thank-you letter is often appreciated. In business world, a thank-you letter has become a must if one cares about his career development or relationship with his business partners.

According to its content and function, thank-you letter can be classified into as many kinds as it can be.

Sample Study

Sample 1: Thank-you letter for hospitality

November 16

Dear Mr. Wilson,

Thank you for your warm hospitality and careful arrangement, which makes our visit to your company rewarding and pleasant.

During the entire visit, my delegation and I were deeply impressed with your staff's enthusiasm, so we enjoyed this business trip very much. Besides, the discussion that you have arranged for us is very fruitful. I am sure this visit will help further expand our business cooperation and make bilateral relations closer.

Once again many thanks for your warm reception. I am waiting for your next visit to our company.

Yours sincerely,

Andy Wu

Market Manager

Sample 2: Thank-you letter for support

May 21

Dear Mr. Wooden,

I am writing to thank you for your financial support to our staff's technical training in the U.S.A.

The fifteen technical workers who will operate at the newly-introduced production line are now under an intensive English course. They will be sent to your company to receive a two-month technical training when their English is good enough.

We would like to thank you again for your generosity and support. We wish this program would become smooth and fruitful.

Yours sincerely,

Thomas Ma

General Manager

Clever Computer Company

Sample 3: Thank-you letter for interview

Dear Miss Catherine,

　　I would like to convey my gratitude to you for interviewing me yesterday about the position of salesperson.

　　I really enjoyed meeting with you and the members of sales department. From our discussion, I strongly feel that you are a very responsible leader. The entire team certainly seems to be highly skilled and full of energy. And the work itself seems rewarding and challenging. I believe that I possess the qualities as a salesperson. I think my education and experience have prepared me well for this position.

　　Thank you again for your interview. I am looking forward to being one member of your company.

Sincerely,
Wilson Song

Sample 4: Thank-you letter for arrangement

September 8

Dear Mr. Steven,

　　I would like to present my sincere thanks for your arrangement to meet your top executive Mr. Henry during our recent visit in Atlanta.

　　Your enthusiasm, competence and creativeness were very impressive. We enjoyed our short stay very much there. It is particularly helpful for us to learn of the technology that is being used in your factories. We have 15 years of experience in manufacturing auto components, so we think that we can fully meet your requirements. We look forward to a mutually beneficial cooperation with you in the near future.

　　Thanks again for your warm reception.

Yours sincerely,
Maggie Chen
Production Manager

Sample Structure

1. Letterhead (if necessary)
2. Date
3. Inside name and address (if necessary)
4. Salutation

5. Body
6. Complimentary close
7. Signature
8. Job title (if necessary)
9. Company, organization (if necessary)
10. Contact way (if necessary)
11. Enclosures (if necessary)

Body Structure

The body usually consists of the following three parts.

1. Opening
2. Middle
3. Closing

Body Analysis

1. Opening: To express your thanks.

> Thank you for your warm hospitality and careful arrangement, which makes our visit to your company rewarding and pleasant.

2. Middle: To state the reasons for thanks.

> During the entire visit, my delegation and I were deeply impressed with your staff's enthusiasm, so we enjoyed this business trip very much. Besides, the discussion that you have arranged for us is very fruitful. I am sure this visit will help further expand our business cooperation and make bilateral relationships closer.

3. Closing: To express your thanks again as well as wishes or expectations.

> Once again many thanks for your warm reception. I am waiting for your next visit to our company.

Writing Tips

1. Be appropriate. One of the main issues with respect to thank-you letters is to know

when to send one.

2. Be prompt. It is always best to send a thank-you letter as soon as possible after the event for which you are doing the thanking.

3. Make it very clear that it is indeed a thank-you letter and that it pertains to a specific event, situation and/or person.

4. Be short and direct. Get straight to the point and never exceed one page. Thank-you letters should be short, direct, sincere, and to the point.

5. A thank-you letter should be expressed as a heartfelt personal sentiment, even when written in a business situation.

6. Always write your thank-you letter to an individual, not an organization or group. Even if it's a situation where a group is involved, write your letter to the senior person in the group and/or the group spokesperson.

7. Make sure you carefully check your spelling and grammar. There's no quicker way to blow your credibility and sincerity than to misspell someone's name.

Useful Expressions

1. Thank you very much for giving me the opportunity for an interview.

非常感谢您给予的面试机会。

2. I am writing to express my thanks for your hospitality during my recent visit to your factory.

兹去函,对您在我最近参观贵工厂期间所给予的热情款待表示感谢。

3. We sincerely (deeply/warmly/truly/really) appreciate the continued support from you.

我们诚挚地感谢您长期以来的支持。

4. I would like to express my deep appreciation for your careful arrangement on my visit to your university.

拜访贵校期间,对您做出的周到安排,我表示深深的谢意。

5. Please accept my sincere (deep/warm/true/real) thanks for your time and effort.

对您所付出的时间及精力,请接受我诚挚的谢意。

6. We are grateful that you can share with us your successful experience.

非常感谢您能与我们分享成功的经验。

7. I must write to say how much I appreciate what you have done for me during my internship in your company.

我必须写信向您表达我是多么感激您为我在贵公司实习时所做的一切。

8. I hope that I will be able to return your hospitality in the near future.

希望在不久的将来,我能回报您们的热情款待。

9. Please give my regards to all the colleagues who prepared this evening party.

请代我向准备此次晚宴的各位同仁表示感谢。

10. During the entire visit, my delegation and I were impressive with your enthusiasm.

在整个访问期间,你们的热情给我及团队代表们都留下了深刻的印象。

11. I sincerely hope we could have more exchanges so that we can continue expanding our bilateral economic and trade relations.

我真诚地希望双方能有更多的交流,以便继续拓展彼此的经贸关系。

12. Thank you for your order and the cheque that were enclosed with this letter.

感谢您随函所附的订单及支票。

13. Thank you again for your wonderful hospitality and I am looking forward to seeing you in the coming future.

再次感谢您的盛情款待,期待着不久的将来能再次见到您。

14. I would like to thank you again for your generous support in my pursuit of education.

再次感谢您在我求学期间对我的慷慨支持。

15. Once again, many thanks for what you have done for us.

再次感谢您为我们所做的一切。

Task Solving

After studying what has been presented above, you may know how to compose a thank-you letter successfully.

Consolidation Exercise

1. Please fill in the blanks according to the initial letter.

Dear Mr. Bob,

　　I am Alice, the General Manager of New Star Company. It is my (1) p_____ to send you a letter of thanks, and I hope this finds you well.

　　I would like to take this moment to (2) e_____ our heartfelt gratitude for the outstanding support your company have offered for us. The (3) c_____ between our two companies has been nothing short of exceptional, and we are (4) e_____ grateful for the trust and commitment you have shown towards our business. Your (5) u_____ support and guidance have been instrumental in our success. As we are (6) e_____ the New Year, we are excited about the opportunities that (7) l_____ ahead and the potential for further growth. We are confident that we will make (8) g_____ achievements together.

Thank you once again for your trust and support. We look forward to a (9) p_____ New Year filled with opportunities for (10) m_____ growth and success.

Alice
General Manager
New Star Company

2. Please translate the English underlined into Chinese.

Dear Mr. Lucas,

(1) <u>I am writing to express my heartfelt gratitude for your exceptional assistance</u> in procuring our company's urgently needed production equipment during our recent trip to France.

Your precious support and tireless efforts throughout the entire process were truly invaluable. From the initial stages of consultation and ordering to arranging shipment, customs clearance, and delivery, (2) <u>you provided us with outstanding service and professional guidance every step</u>. Your knowledge and expertise were crucial in ensuring that the process ran smoothly, and (3) <u>your friendly attitude and great patience made the entire experience a pleasure</u>. Furthermore, your thoughtful arrangement to provide us with a tour of France's famous attractions during our leisure time was truly touching. (4) <u>It was a pleasure to experience the culture and beautiful attractions of your country.</u>

On behalf of the Wilson Company, (5) <u>I would like to express my sincere thanks once again for everything you have done</u> to make our trip a success. I look forward to the opportunity to cooperate with you again in the future.

Sincerely,
Steven Wan
General Manager
Wilson Company

3. Please translate the Chinese in the brackets into English.

March 15

Dear Mr. Adams,

On behalf of our company, _____ (感谢您的热情款待) during the Asia-Pacific Science and Invention Exhibition. _____ (在整个活动过程中，因为您的努力与帮助), this exhibition can be accomplished successfully. And _____ (您所做的一切使得展会顺利进行). Besides that, _____ (为展会所做的精心安排和准备) are greatly conducive to our business expansion.

_____（再次感谢您周到的服务）. I am looking forward to seeing you at next exhibition.

Sincerely,
Harrison

Writing Practice

Directions: Supposing you are Susan and you have just been interviewed for the position of HR assistant by Mr. Smith, the HR Manager of Guangzhou Evergreen Trade Company. During the interview, you receive a warm reception. Therefore you want to write a thank-you letter to Mr. Smith. The hints are as follows.

1. Express your thanks to Mr. Smith;
2. Present the reasons for thanks;
3. Tell him that you are interested in the position;
4. Enclose the application form that he gave you;
5. Express your thanks again and expectations.

Task 5   Congratulation Letter

Learning Objectives

• Learn about the definition, function and types of congratulation letter.
• Be familiar with the structure, content and format of congratulation letter.
• Master the useful expressions such as words, phrases and sentences for congratulation letter.
• Be able to skillfully compose a correct congratulation letter in the real business situation.

Task Situation

Yesterday (August 10), Mr. Stephen learned about the news that Miss Angel was promoted to the general manager of her company. To express his congratulations to her, Mr. Stephen asked Mabel to compose a congratulation letter to Miss Angel in his name.

Supposing you are Mabel, how do you finish the task assigned to you?

Questions

• What basic contents are included in a congratulation letter?
• How are the structure and format of a congratulation letter?
• What points should we pay attention to when composing a congratulation letter?

Theory Background

A congratulation letter is a letter written to deliver a congratulatory message to one's customers, business associates, colleagues, relatives, friends, etc. for starting a new business, establishing a branch, being promoted, getting a new job, graduating or other significant events or occasions. Congratulation letter is a good way not only to maintain business relations with your customers but also to make the relationship of this kind much closer.

According to its function and situation used in, congratulation letter can be classified into as many kinds as it can be.

Sample Study

Sample 1: Congratulation letter on promotion

Evan's Clothes Trading Company
No. 68, Guangzhou Avenue, Guangzhou
Tel: 020-××××　××××
Fax: 020-××××　××××
Email: evans@sina.com
Website:evanstc@yahoo.com

January 28
Mr. Miller
Douglas Clothes Company Ltd.
No. 988, Ivory Street, New York
Tel: 987-×××××
Email: douglascct@yahoo.com

Dear Mr. Miller,

  How happy we are feeling when we have learned of your promotion to marketing manager from your company's website. We are writing to extend our sincere congratulations to you.

  We are delighted that your work and achievement in the past decades have been recognized and appreciated. We are also very pleased that your effort and persistence have been rewarded. Through the years of cooperating with you, we are quite aware of how hard you have been working and how much you have been dedicated to your company. In addition, we are deeply impressed with the great contribution that you have made to your company.

  Congratulations on your promotion once again and best wishes for more advancement in your new position. We are awaiting your visit to our company next month.

Yours sincerely,
Shelly Lee
General Manager
Evan's Clothes Trading Company

Sample 2: Congratulation letter on starting business

May 15

Dear Mr. Kelvin,

  I have learned with delight that you are starting your own advertising company and starting business today. I would like to offer my warm congratulations to you on this significant event.

  You have been specializing in advertisement business for many years and have gained great popularity in business circles of advertisement. Your rich work experience and unique insights into advertising are sure to bring greater development to your newly-established company.

  Please accept my heartiest congratulations to you again. I sincerely wish your new company runs smoothly and look forward to further cooperation with you in the near future.

Faithfully yours,
Cathy

Sample 3: Congratulation letter on establishing new branch

Dear Mr. Clark,

  I have learned with delight that you are establishing a new branch in London. Please accept my utmost congratulations on the opening of your London branch.

  Due to your brilliant background and rich experience, we wish you every success in your increased involvement in the competitive market.

  Should there be any way in which we can offer assistance, please do not hesitate to contact me personally. I am looking forward to close cooperation with you in the development of business.

Yours sincerely,
Mike Tang

Sample 4: Congratulation letter on winning honor

November 13

Dear Miss Betty,

  Congratulations!

  I am pleased to congratulate you and your team for winning the Excellent Performance Award for the current year. On behalf of Bright Life Insurance, I would like to congratulate you for the great accomplishment.

> Your team has been the leading performer, and has achieved best rankings for customer satisfaction and annual sales target. You have certainly set the benchmark for other teams to achieve. In recognition of your efforts, we have decided to reward your team with $2,000 per person for the current quarter.
>
> I am sure, your team will continue to perform in the same fashion, and raise the standards to new levels.
>
> Sincerely yours,
Catherine Tang

Sample 5: Congratulation letter on anniversary

> Dear Mr. Clark,
>
> November 12 is the 25th anniversary of the establishment of your company. On this significant occasion, on behalf of Guangzhou Double Trade Company, hereby I extend my cordial congratulations to your company and to all its executives and staff members.
>
> And I would like to take this opportunity to express my heartfelt gratitude to you for your cooperation and support over the past years.
>
> May your company perform better and grow faster!
>
> Yours sincerely,
Austin Joe
General Manager
Guangzhou Double Trade Company

Sample Structure

> 1. Letterhead (if necessary)
> 2. Date
> 3. Inside name and address (if necessary)
> 4. Salutation
> 5. Body
> 6. Complimentary close
> 7. Signature
> 8. Job title (if necessary)
> 9. Company, organization (if necessary)
> 10. Contact method (if necessary)
> 11. Enclosures (if necessary)

Body Structure

The body usually consists of the following three parts.

1. Opening
2. Middle
3. Closing

 Body Analysis

1. Opening: To state the information source as well as the purpose for writing.

How happy we are feeling when we have learned of your promotion to marketing manager from your company's website. We are writing to extend our sincere congratulations to you.

2. Middle: To state the reasons for congratulations.

We are delighted that your work and achievement in the past decades have been recognized and appreciated. We are also very pleased that your effort and persistence have been rewarded.

3. Closing: To express your congratulations again as well as wishes or expectations.

Congratulations on your promotion once again and best wishes for your more advancement in your new position. We are awaiting your visit to our company next month.

 Writing Tips

1. Write the congratulation letter as soon as possible after the fortunate event takes place.
2. State in the beginning the specific occasion that has motivated you to write a congratulation letter.
3. Express praise and approval of the reader's accomplishment in your congratulation letter.
4. Keep your congratulation letter simple and concise—under one page in length.
5. Keep your letter positive and don't include any negative comments or unhappy news.
6. The tone of a congratulation letter should be sincere, natural, positive and without exaggeration.
7. Don't exaggerate your congratulatory words or your letter may seem sarcastic or mocking.

8. Edit the letter for correct structure, grammar, spelling and punctuation, etc. before sending it.

Useful Expressions

1. I am writing you to deliver our sincerest congratulations on your promotion to general manager of your company.

兹去函,对您晋升为贵公司总经理表示最衷心的祝贺。

2. On the happy occasion of your company's 20th anniversary, I would like to extend my hearty congratulations.

在贵公司成立20周年庆典之际,谨此献上我衷心的祝贺。

3. Please accept our heartfelt congratulations on your establishing a new branch.

衷心祝贺贵公司成立分公司。

4. I would like to take this opportunity to congratulate you on your appointment to the director of Tina Group.

借此机会,恭祝您被任命为蒂纳集团的董事。

5. We would like to express my wholehearted congratulations on relocating your factory to a new site.

衷心祝贺贵工厂乔迁。

6. We take pleasure in presenting our congratulations on your products receiving "Fine Quality Brand Award" of this year.

我们非常高兴地恭贺贵公司产品荣获本年度"优质品牌奖"。

7. I sincerely congratulate you on being successfully admitted to Harvard University and receiving a full scholarship.

我衷心祝贺您被哈佛大学录取,并获得全额奖学金。

8. I warmly congratulate you on successful graduation from Yale University with a Doctor Degree of Business Administration.

热烈祝贺您从耶鲁大学毕业并获工商管理博士学位。

9. We feel proud of your unparalleled achievements and you really deserve this award.

我们为您所取得的无与伦比的成就感到骄傲,获此奖项您当之无愧。

10. We really think that your promotion is richly deserved because of your outstanding contributions to your company.

我们认为您的晋升实至名归,因为您为贵公司做出了突出贡献。

11. We are delighted that your effort has been recognized and your persistence has been rewarded in the past five years at last.

我们高兴的是,您过去五年的努力最终得到了认可,您的坚持最终获得了回报。

12. We are deeply impressed with the significant achievement that you have made during

the past fifteen years.

您在过去十五年里取得的辉煌成就给我们留下了深刻的印象。

13. We are quite aware of how hard you have been working and how much you've been dedicated to your company.

我们非常清楚您工作是多么勤勤恳恳,对公司是多么尽职尽责。

14. With your rich experience and proven capability in this filed, I am sure you will make much more progress in the future.

以您在这一行业丰富的经验以及业已证明的实力,我相信您将来会取得更大的进步。

15. Congratulations to you again and best wishes for your continued progress in your new position in the years to come.

再次恭喜您,并祝愿您将来在新的工作岗位上继续进步。

16. I heartily convey my best wishes for your success and look forward to a closer cooperation with you in the near future.

衷心祝贺您取得成功,并期待在不久的将来与您进一步合作。

17. We cordially wish your company would achieve an even greater achievement in the new century.

我们衷心地祝愿贵公司在新世纪能取得更大的成就。

18. I congratulate you again on this honor from the bottom of my heart, and wish you the best of luck in all of your future endeavors.

再次衷心地祝贺您获此荣誉,并祝您未来好运连连。

19. Please accept our true congratulations on your promotion once again and wish you make a greater success in the future.

对于您的晋升,请再次接受我们真诚的祝贺,并祝你在将来取得更大的成功。

20. We would like to sincerely congratulate you again on your new company's starting business.

我们再次衷心地祝贺您的新公司开业。

 Task Solving

After studying what has been presented above, you may know how to compose a congratulation letter successfully.

 Consolidation Exercise

1. Please fill in the blanks according to the initial letter.

> Dear Mr. Black,
>   I am writing to express my heartfelt congratulations on the establishment of your new (1) b_____ in Boston.

Module 4　Writing for Business Etiquette

　　This is a momentous (2) o_____ for your company, (3) m_____ a significant milestone in the development of your company and a (4) t_____ to the strength of your company as well.
　　We are (5) p_____ to be business partner with you and (6) e_____ about the opportunities this new development brings.
　　On (7) b_____ of Sunshine Group, I offer my (8) s_____ congratulations on this new chapter in your journey. May your success in Boston be as (9) f_____ as it has been in the past. We look forward to (10) s_____ further cooperation between us in the years to come.

Sincerely yours,
Hunter
Sunshine Group

2. Please translate the English underlined into Chinese.

Dear Mr. Wang,
　　I am writing to (1) <u>extend my sincere congratulations on your major order recently signed</u> with the Saudi government, one of the countries from the One Belt and One Road, valued at $200 million.
　　As a long-standing partner of the Guangzhou Super Foreign Trade Company, I am extremely proud to witness your remarkable success. Your company's (2) <u>good reputation, exceptional product quality and superb after-sales service</u> have all contributed significantly to this accomplishment. Your company's (3) <u>dedication and commitment to providing first-rate services and products</u> have paid off in this landmark contract.
　　(4) <u>Once again, I offer my warmest congratulations to you and your team</u> for this remarkable milestone. I am confident that your company will (5) <u>remain as prosperous as ever and achieve even greater heights in the future</u>.

Faithfully,
Austin Joe
General Manager
Guangzhou Overseas Trading Company

3. Please translate the Chinese in the brackets into English.

Dear Mr. Michael,
　　I take great pleasure in _____
(向您致以最热烈的祝贺) on you awarded "Employee of This Year" in your company when I read of the exciting news from your company's website.

I am not a little surprised and _____
_____(这的确是您应得的荣誉). I know _____
_____(花费了大量的时间和精力)on your work. And I am really impressed with your strict self-discipline and great self-sacrifice spirit. Now _____
_____(您曾经付出的努力最终得到了回报).

Congratulations to you again. I sincerely wish _____
_____(您在不久的将来取得更大的成功).

Yours faithfully,
George
General Manager

 Writing Practice

Directions: Mr. John Smith was promoted to the general manager of Guangzhou Sunflower E-commerce Co., Ltd. You are Edward Jackson, the general manager of Shanghai Grand Shoes Production Company. You both are cooperative business partners as well as good friends. Please write a congratulation letter to Mr. John Smith on his promotion. The hints are as follows.

1. Telling him how you know the information;
2. Congratulating him on his promotion;
3. Highlighting his ability in some aspect;
4. Congratulating him on his promotion once again.

Task 6   Reservation Letter

 Learning Objectives

- Learn about the definition, function and types of reservation letter.
- Be familiar with the structure, content and format of reservation letter.
- Master the useful expressions such as words, phrases and sentences for reservation letter.
- Be able to skillfully compose a correct reservation letter in the real business situation.

 Task Situation

Mr. Stephen accepts Mr. Henry's invitation and is going to pay a business visit to America Fox Trade Company on August 4, Monday. Today (July 18) he asks Mabel to help him book a ticket from China Southern Airlines. The booking details are as follows.

Time and date: 10:00 a.m.; August 3
Flight No.: SA 2248
Flight class: First-class
Seat preference: A window seat between Row 4 to 7
Way of paying: Master Card

Supposing you are Mabel, how do you finish the task assigned to you?

 Questions

- What basic contents are included in a reservation letter?
- How are the structure and format of a reservation letter?
- What points should we pay attention to when composing a reservation letter?

 Theory Background

Reservation letter is a letter written to reserve tickets, dinner table, hotel rooms, conference rooms, etc. for the purposes of business meeting, business travel, business entertaining, personal leisure and so on.

Whatever the reservation may be, it is important to give the person involved detailed information such as departure time/date/place, arrival time/date/place, stay duration, special requirements, cultural taboo and so on.

According to its function and situation used in, reservation letter can be classified into as many kinds as it can be.

Sample Study

Sample 1: Reservation letter for hotel room

June 15

Dear Miss Lucy,

 I am Tracy, secretary from Guangzhou New Star Trade Company. Our general manager, Mr. Philip, will be flying to Sydney for a business visit. Therefore I am writing to make a room reservation at your hotel for him.

 The booking details are as follows.

 1. A single room with one large bed

 2. Four nights: July 3 (Sunday) to July 6 (Wednesday)

 3. Room preference: quiet, with a balcony for a spectacular view of the city

 Mr. Philip will arrive at around 10:00 p.m. on the night of July 3, and it could be a little late, but we hope that the room can still be kept available.

 We would be appreciated if you could early confirm our reservation. We are looking forward to receiving your reply very soon.

Sincerely yours,

Tracy

Secretary to General Manager

Guangzhou New Star Trade Company

Sample 2: Reservation letter for restaurant table

August 1

Dear Mr. Black,

 Our company is going to hold a farewell dinner party for guests. I am writing to reserve a table at your restaurant under the name of our general manager, Mr. Smith.

 We would like to book a table for ten persons with a budget of 100 yuan each person excluding drinks. The table should be near the window with a bird-eye view of the lake. Chinese food is preferred and we welcome any special items on the menu to be introduced to us. The dinner will begin at 6:30 p.m. on August 21, Monday, lasting for about one hour and a half.

 We would be grateful if you could give us your confirmation at your convenience and we are looking forward to your early reply.

Yours sincerely,

Emily

Sample 3: Reservation letter for air ticket

April 16

Dear Mr. Peter,

    I am Cathy, the secretary to sales manager of Guangzhou Rainbow Trading Company. I would like to book a flight to Australia on May 18 (Tuesday), first class and round trip for our sales manager, Mr. Albert.

    He will be leaving at 10:00 a.m. on that day and return at 8:00 a.m. on May 30. Bank of China (Guangzhou Baiyun Branch) has been instructed to pay the fare, and please submit your account to them directly. Enclosed is a check of RMB 2,500, representing the deposit for the ticket.

    I would feel obliged if you could send me an e-mail at gzrainbow@sina.com or call at 020-×××× ×××× confirming my reservation as soon as possible.

Yours cordially,

Cathy

Secretary to Sales Manager

Guangzhou Rainbow Trading Company

Sample 4: Reservation letter for a product display venue

August 8

Dear Sir or Madam,

    On behalf of the Foremost Group, we would like to reserve a suitable venue at your conference center for our group to release two new smartphone models on August 14.

    In order to provide our customers and media attendees with an unforgettable experience, we need a space that can accommodate approximately 500 people, including seating areas and a product display section. We would like the seating area to be spacious enough to allow our guests to sit comfortably and view the launch event. Additionally, we need a product display area that is large enough to showcase our new products effectively, as well as three wireless microphones and a large projection screen.

    We will be highly appreciated if we could receive your response before August 11. Look forward to your early confirmation and your willingness to consider our request to host our upcoming product launch event at your conference center.

Sincerely yours,

Maggie

Secretary

Foremost Group

Sample Structure

1. Letterhead (if necessary)
2. Date
3. Inside name and address (if necessary)
4. Salutation
5. Body
6. Complimentary close
7. Signature
8. Job title (if necessary)
9. Company, organization (if necessary)
10. Contact method (if necessary)
11. Enclosures (if necessary)

 Body Structure

The body usually consists of the following three parts.

1. Opening
2. Middle
3. Closing

 Body Analysis

1. Opening: To state the reasons for reserving as well as the purpose for writing and show your identification sometimes.

> I am Tracy, a secretary from Guangzhou New Star Trade Company. Our general manager, Mr. Philip, will be flying to Sydney for a business visit. Therefore I am writing to make a room reservation at your hotel for him.

2. Middle: To provide detailed reserving information such as time, place, special requirements and so on.

> The booking details are as follows.
> 1. A single room with one large bed
> 2. Four nights: July 3 (Sunday) to July 6 (Wednesday)
> ...

> Mr. Philip will arrive at around 10:00 p.m. on the night of July 3, and it could be a little late, but we hope that the room can still be kept available.

3. Closing: To express your thanks as well as your wishes or expectations.

> We would be appreciated if you could early confirm our reservation. We are looking forward to receiving your reply very soon.

Writing Tips

1. Be brief, straight forward, concise and complete when writing a reservation letter.

2. It should specifically state what you need and how the payment will be made.

3. Cover all details like the date and time of arrival, complete contact details, type of room, stay duration, etc.

4. Provide complete details to the reader so that there is no misunderstanding or confusion.

5. The reservation letter should be short but with complete information.

6. Mention if you have any special needs like the medical condition or any requirement for an internet connection, etc.

7. Avoid usage of slang or messaging language, as that does not indicate professionalism.

8. Close the letter by thanking and giving your complete contact details.

Useful Expressions

1. I would like to reserve an air ticket to Paris on January 8 on Air France, first class and round trip.

我要预订一张前往巴黎的机票,1月8日,法国航空公司,头等舱,双程。

2. I am writing to book a flight for Beijing at 17:30 a.m. on December 4.

兹去函:预订12月4日17:30飞往北京的航班。

3. We would like to make a reservation for a lecture hall equipped with a computer, a projector and four wireless microphones.

我们想预订一间带电脑、投影仪和4个无线麦克风的报告厅。

4. We would like to book a double room with a balcony overlooking the sea at your hotel for 4 nights starting from June 8.

我们想在贵酒店预订一间带阳台的海景双人房,自6月8日起,共计4晚。

5. I would like to reserve a table for ten with a budget of 100 yuan a person excluding drinks in your hotel under the name of Mr. Black.

我想以布莱克先生的名义,在贵酒店预订一张十人餐桌,预算是每人100元,不含酒水。

6. I would like to reserve a single room for 5 nights starting from August 7.

我想预订一间单人房,8月7日入住,住5晚。

7. The departure time is at 6:00 p.m. on December 7 and the arrival time is at 9:00 p.m. on that day.

出发时间是12月7日下午6点,到达时间是当日晚上9点。

8. How much is a one-way airplane ticket to New York?

到纽约的单程机票多少钱?

9. Is there a special rate for a group reservation?

团体预定是否有优惠?

10. Can I pay my room charge with a credit card?

我能用信用卡付房费吗?

11. Do you have a transfer service from airport to hotel free of charge?

请问贵酒店有没有免费接机服务?

12. We may arrive a little late, but please keep our reservation.

我们可能会晚点到,但请保留我们的预定。

13. Should you have any questions, please do not hesitate to contact us.

如有任何疑问,请随时与我们联系。

14. Please let us know the relevant information such as cost for drinks and desserts by early e-mail reply.

请尽早通过电子邮件告知我们相关信息,如酒水费用、甜品费用。

15. I would be very obliged if you could write back to me confirming my reservation as soon as possible.

如您能尽快回信确认我的预订,我将不胜感激。

16. We are looking forward to receiving your early confirmation.

我们期待早日收到您的确认。

17. Please send me a written confirmation letter for my reservation by October 11.

请在10月11日前为我邮寄一份书面的预订确认函。

18. We hope to receive your confirmation letter before August 5 if possible.

如有可能,我希望在8月5日前收到贵方的确认函。

Task Solving

After studying what has been presented above, you may know how to compose a reservation letter successfully.

Module 4 Writing for Business Etiquette

 Consolidation Exercise

1. Please fill in the blanks according to the initial letter.

Dear London Hilton Hotel,

　　I am Cathy, a (1) s_____ of Shanghai East Trading Company. I am writing to (2) m_____ a reservation at your hotel for Henry, our General Manager.

　　Mr. Henry will be (3) a_____ at London Heathrow Airport at 11:00 a.m. and he will (4) s_____ at your hotel from November 5 to November 10.

　　The reservation details are as follows.

　　1. A room with a (5) c_____ bed, quiet atmosphere and (6) o_____ of the city.

　　2. Provide (7) f_____ breakfast for Mr. Henry and other guests that (8) a_____ him.

　　3. A private car to (9) p_____ Mr. Henry up from the airport to the hotel on November 5.

　　Thank you for your time and (10) c_____. We look forward to your early reply.

　　　　　　　　　　　　　　　　　　　　　　　　　　　　Sincerely yours,
　　　　　　　　　　　　　　　　　　　　　　　　　　　　Cathy

2. Please translate the English underlined into Chinese.

September 10

Dear Sir or Madam,

　　(1) <u>I am writing to make a reservation for five high-speed train tickets</u> from Guangzhou to Guiyang, Guizhou. (2) <u>We plan to take a trip one week before the National Day holiday</u>, so we need a train schedule that is available during that time frame.

　　We value the travel experience greatly, so we would appreciate (3) <u>if you could try to book the seats for us in the same carriage</u>. If possible, (4) <u>we would also like the seats to be as close together as possible</u> so that we can easily chat and enjoy the journey.

　　For payment method, we choose to use online payment on Alipay. (5) <u>If you would like to get any more information or have any questions</u>, please feel free to contact us. We look forward to hearing from your early confirmation.

　　　　　　　　　　　　　　　　　　　　　　　　　　　　Sincerely yours,
　　　　　　　　　　　　　　　　　　　　　　　　　　　　Miss Mary

3. Please translate the Chinese in the brackets into English.

April 18

Dear Sir,

    I am Huang Li, secretary of Sunshine Clothes Company. I'm writing to _____ (在贵酒店预订一间会议室) for next Monday, October 19. We hope that _____ (该会议室足够大，能够容纳150人) and _____ (提供多媒体设备). In addition, we hope that your hotel can _____ (提供午餐及酒水服务).

    We would be highly appreciated if you could _____ (早日对我们的预定予以确认).

Sincerely yours,
Huang Li

Writing Practice

Directions: Catherine is secretary of HLD Information and Communication Company. Her company is going to hold a technology seminar from May 10 to May 11. Mr. Black, the general manager, asks her to write a letter to make a reservation in Hilton Hotel. The hints are as follows.

1. 带浴室的双人房18间，3晚
2. 可容纳35人的会议室1间，2天
3. 到达时间：5月9日下午5:30
4. 离开时间：5月12日上午10:00
5. 想了解酒店的房价、会议室的租金及膳食服务等情况
6. 希望尽早得到答复

Task 7 Complaint Letter

 Learning Objectives

- Learn about the definition, function and types of complaint letter.
- Be familiar with the structure, content and format of complaint letter.
- Master the useful expressions such as words, phrases and sentences for complaint letter.
- Be able to skillfully compose a correct complaint letter in the real business situation.

 Task Situation

Mabel had a business trip in Beijing last Friday on August 26 and she stayed in Holiday Inn Hotel, but she had an unhappy experience during her stay in the hotel. The problems are as follows.

1. Reception staff's bad service
2. The air-conditioner was not cold enough
3. The bathroom was dirty and the water was over hot
4. The loud noise at night

Supposing you are Mabel, how do you write the complaint letter?

 Questions

- What basic contents are included in a complaint letter?
- How are the structure and format of a complaint letter?
- What points should we pay attention to when composing a complaint letter?

 Theory Background

The complaint letter is a letter written to complain about something unhappy or unsatisfying to a person or a business. It is usually used for expressing dissatisfaction with bad service, unpleasant experience, poor quality, etc. and presenting a solution. It must be noted that we should be objective, polite and persuasive when describing the problems. Our purpose for complaint is to solve the problems instead of making them complicated.

According to its content and function, complaint letter can be classified into as many kinds as it can be.

Sample Study

Sample 1: Complaint letter for goods damage

July 27

Dear Miss Emma,

We have received the consignment shipped by S.S. "Flying Fish" with thanks. But after a careful examination, we find there is something wrong with the goods, so we are writing to make a complaint to you.

When we unpack the cartons, we find Carton No.21, No.115 and No.163 are broken and the goods are exposed in the open air with scratches on the surface of each item.

Though the damaged goods can still be sold, the price will be much lower than that in perfect condition. Therefore, we suggest you give us a 50% discount on the original price, or we will have to return them to you. The extra freight, of course, will be for your account.

Your consideration to our advice will be highly appreciated. We earnestly wish to receive your solutions to this matter as soon as possible.

Yours truly,

David Smith

Enc.: Survey report

Sample 2: Complaint letter for poor quality

January 2

Dear Mr. Hunter,

I am Shelly, a customer of your store. Now I am writing to complain about the poor quality of the goods I bought last Monday.

I bought an electronic dictionary from your store online on January 1, but I find it has some problems after using it for a short period of time. First, the battery needs recharging after a mere 2 hours of use. This means that I need to carry a charger with me wherever I go. Second, the buttons on the electronic dictionary are so small that it is nearly impossible to type anything with them. Personally, I find this completely unacceptable. Therefore, I would like you to either change it for another model that works well or return me a full refund for it.

Your consideration is greatly appreciated. I am looking forward to your early reply.

Yours sincerely,

Shelly

Sample 3: Complaint letter for wrong delivery

May 13

Dear Mr. Wang,

  Referring to our Order No. 26, you have delivered some wrong goods, which arrived at Bangkok on May 12.

  We appreciate your prompt delivery. But, when opening Case No.14, we found that it contained totally different items, which we had not ordered. We assume that a mistake may have been made in assembling the order. All other items are correct and in good condition.

  As the items we have ordered are needed urgently, please dispatch the missing articles at once. We enclose a list of detailed description about the items that should have been in Case No.14. Please check this with our order and your copy of the invoice.

  Your prompt consideration to our advice will be highly appreciated. We earnestly wish to receive your solutions to this matter as soon as possible.

Faithfully yours,
Johnson Black

Sample 4: Complaint letter for short delivery

February 6

Dear Ms. Yang,

  I am writing to inform you that the goods we ordered from your company have not been supplied correctly.

  On January 25, we placed an order for 1,100 mini fans. The consignment arrived yesterday but contained only 1,000 mini fans.

  This error put us in a difficult position, as we had to make some emergency purchases to fulfill our commitments to all our customers. This caused us considerable inconvenience.

  We would like you to make up the shortfall immediately and ensure that such errors do not happen again. Otherwise, we may have to look elsewhere for our supplies.

  I look forward to hearing from you in return.

Yours sincerely,
Charlie
Purchasing Officer

Sample Structure

1. Letterhead (if necessary)
2. Date
3. Inside name and address (if necessary)
4. Salutation
5. Body
6. Complimentary close
7. Signature
8. Job title (if necessary)
9. Company, organization (if necessary)
10. Contact way (if necessary)
11. Enclosures (if necessary)

Body Structure

The body usually consists of the following three parts.

1. Opening
2. Middle
3. Closing

Body Analysis

1. Opening: To state the purpose for writing and show your identification sometimes.

> We have received the consignment shipped by S.S. "Flying Fish" with thanks. But after a careful examination, we find there is something wrong with the goods, so we are writing to make a complaint to you.

2. Middle: To state the reasons for your complaint and provide solutions to the matter.

> When we unpack the cartons, we find Carton No.21, No.115 and No.163 are broken and the goods are exposed in the open air with scratches on the surface of each item.
>
> Though the damaged goods can still be sold, the price will be much lower than that in perfect condition. Therefore, we suggest you give us a 50% discount on the original price, or we will have to return them to you. The extra freight, of course, will be for your account.

3. Closing: To express your thanks as well as your wishes or expectations.

> Your consideration to our advice will be highly appreciated. We earnestly wish to receive your solutions to this matter as soon as possible.

Writing Tips

1. Present the problems with details such as the relevant facts, dates, names, and details.

2. State exactly what you want to be done about the problem and when you expect your complaint to be resolved.

3. Express confidence that your complaint letter will be addressed promptly and the problem settled satisfactorily.

4. Include all documents regarding your problem and be sure to send copies, not originals.

5. Write your letter with a friendly and complimentary tone and avoid writing an angry, sarcastic, or threatening letter.

6. Make your letter brief and to the point, and keep a copy of the letter for your records.

Useful Expressions

1. I am writing to complain about the quality of your products.
现写信向贵方投诉产品质量问题。

2. I would like to express my complaint about the shoes that I bought in your shop last Saturday.
我想表达我对上周六在贵店所购买的鞋子的不满。

3. I really must complain about the quality of the goods that you recently sent us.
对于贵方最近发出的货物存在的质量问题,我必须向您投诉。

4. We regret to inform you that the goods shipped per S.S "Peace" arrived in such an unsatisfactory condition.
我们遗憾地通知贵方,由"和平"轮装运的货物抵达时状况令人不满。

5. We felt very disappointed with your salesclerk's poor service when I was shopping at your shop mall.
昨天在贵商场购物时,我对销售员糟糕的服务表示非常失望。

6. We regret that we found that twenty of computers were badly damaged when we unpacked the bags yesterday.
很遗憾,当我们昨天打开袋子的时候,发现其中有20台电脑严重损毁。

7. It is a great pity that we find that there is something wrong with the components of the washing machine.

非常遗憾,我们发现洗衣机的零件有问题。

8. On checking, we discovered that there were 10 cases of socks missing.

经检查,我们发现有10箱袜子不见了。

9. The quality of the goods that you supplied far falls/is far below the standard as expected.

贵方提供的物品质量远远未能达到期望的标准。

10. I regret to say that five of boxes were found to be in a badly damaged condition. This was apparently attributable to faulty packing.

遗憾的是,我们发现其中5箱严重损毁。很明显这是包装不慎造成的。

11. Apparently, the problems of goods quality were caused during the transportation.

显然,产品质量问题是在运输过程中产生的。

12. After a closer examination, we found the damage was caused by roughly handling.

经检查发现,损毁是由粗暴处理造成的。

13. The delay of goods was due to poor weather conditions.

发货延误是恶劣天气导致的。

14. We should be obliged if you would replace the wrong goods you delivered with the correct ones.

贵方若能更换发错的货物,我们将不胜感激。

15. We should be grateful if you would give us a complete refund for the defective goods.

对于这批瑕疵货物,贵方若能全数退还货款,我们将不胜感激。

16. We hope that you can examine the goods carefully and reply to us in time.

我们希望您能仔细检查货物并及时回复我们。

17. We will appreciate it if you could look into the matter and let us know your disposal.

如果您能调查此事并告知您的处理意见,我们将不胜感激。

18. Your prompt solution and consideration will be highly appreciated.

如您能及时解决问题,我们将不胜感谢。

19. I do hope that the problems will be solved as soon as possible.

我的确希望问题能尽快得到解决。

20. I would appreciate it if you would look into the matter.

如果你们能对事件进行调查,本人将不胜感谢。

 Task Solving

After studying what has been presented above, you may know how to compose a complaint letter successfully.

Module 4 Writing for Business Etiquette

 Consolidation Exercise

1. Please fill in the blanks according to the initial letter.

May 15
Dear Customer Center,

We have received the phones (1) o_____ online from your company and regret to find there are something (2) w_____ with some of them. Now we are writing to (3) c_____ to you.

Firstly, some phone screens are badly (4) s_____. And the damage appears to have been (5) c_____ by roughly packing. Secondly, some phone battery life is significantly (6) s_____ than that stated in instruction. Even in standby mode, the batteries drain very quickly. We were (7) d_____ that the phone's performance does not meet our expectations, so we would like you to either return a full (8) r_____ to me or replace the defective ones with new goods.

We have been a (9) l_____ customer of your company for many years. We will be grateful for you if you could (10) a_____ the above problems. We are waiting for your immediate reply.

Yours sincerely,
Venus

2. Please translate the English underlined into Chinese.

Dear Miss Wendy,

I am writing to (1) <u>express my dissatisfaction with my recent experience at your hotel</u>.

As a five-star hotel, I believe that the level of (2) <u>service and facilities provided should meet customers' expectations</u>. However, I found that the breakfast served were limited in variety and did not meet my expectations for a five-star hotel. Additionally, in a first tier city, (3) <u>the swimming pool closed as early as 9:00 p.m.</u>, which was a bit surprising to me. I understand that there may be circumstances that contribute to these issues, but I believe that they should be addressed in a timely manner to (4) <u>ensure the satisfaction of every distinguished guests</u>. As a regular customer, I expect nothing less than the best experience when choosing your hotel.

I hope that my feedback will be taken seriously and that (5) <u>necessary measures will be taken to address these concerns</u>. I look forward to a positive resolution to these matters and thank you for your time and attention to this matter.

Sincerely,
Susan Li

3. Please translate the Chinese in the brackets into English.

December 5

Dear Miss Morris,

　　_____ (现去函投诉贵公司培训课程) on health and safety that I attended on November 27.

　　When I booked this course, I chose your company as it was highly recommended and the course seemed to be of a high standard. However, it turned out to be the opposite and _____ (我对你们的培训课程感到非常失望).

　　First, the trainer was not as good as expected due to her lack of practical experience.

　　Second, the class was supposed to be about 8 people but in mine there were about 15.

　　Third, I should make it clear that _____ (上课的时间比你们承诺的晚了一个小时).

　　Finally, the lunch served was cold and there were no refreshments served at all.

　　I am sure you can understand my disappointment. _____ (希望你们能立即调查此事). I would be very appreciated if _____ (你们能退回我全部的培训费用). I am looking forward to your early reply.

Yours sincerely,
Tracy
Cabin Attendant
Southern China Airlines

Writing Practice

Directions: Suppose you are Linda, a purchasing manager of Guangzhou Lucas Shoes Company. Your company purchased 2,500 pairs of shoes by mail order from America Perth Shoes Company last month and you found 25 pairs with holes in them and 50 pairs with dirty spots on them when you received the goods yesterday. Now you are writing a complaint letter to Miss Alisa, the sales manager of America Perth Shoes Company.

Module 4　Writing for Business Etiquette

Task 8　Reply Letter to Complaint

 Learning Objectives

• Learn about the definition, function and types of reply letter to complaint.
• Be familiar with the structure, content and format of reply letter to complaint.
• Master the useful expressions such as words, phrases and sentences for reply letter to complaint.
• Be able to skillfully compose a correct reply letter to complaint in the real business situation.

 Task Situation

This morning, Mr. Stephen received a letter complaining about wrong goods from Mr. Leon, market manager of Australia Import and Export Textile Company. The letter is as follows.

November 11
Dear Mr. Stephen,
　　Our Order No. 3 per S.S. "Prince"
　We duly received the documents and took delivery of the goods on arrival of steamship "Prince" at Sydney.
　We thank you for your prompt execution of this order. Everything appears to be correct except in case No. 3.
　Unfortunately when we opened this case, we found it contained completely different articles, and we presume that a mistake must have been made and the contents of this case were for another order.
　As the goods we ordered are greatly needed by our customers, we have to ask you to arrange for the dispatch of replacements at once. We attach a list of the contents of case No. 3, and we shall be appreciated if you will check this with our order and send us your invoice.
　I am looking forward to hearing from you soon.

　　　　　　　　　　　　　　　　　　　　　　　　　　　　　Yours faithfully,
　　　　　　　　　　　　　　　　　　　　　　　　　　　　　Mr. Leon
　　　　　　　　　　　　　　　　　　　　　　　　　　　　　Market Manager

Now, Mr. Stephen asks Mabel to write a reply letter to Mr. Leon in his name. Supposing you are Mabel, how do you finish the task assigned to you?

Questions

- What basic contents are included in a reply letter to complaint?
- How are the structure and format of a reply letter to complaint?
- What points should we pay attention to when composing a reply letter to complaint?

Theory Background

Reply letters to complaint are written to answer the complaint about something unhappy or unsatisfying to somebody. They are also called adjustment letters—to adjust a difficult situation to the benefit of both the writer and the reader. Reply letters to complaint must be prompt.

In business situation, one may complain about the poor service, wrong delivery, delayed delivery, damaged goods, defective goods, inferior quality, short weight, etc., so a reply letter to complaint must be written to explain and apologize for the wrong doings so that the problems can be settled smoothly and successfully.

According to its content and function, it can be classified into as many kinds as it can be.

Sample Study

Sample 1: Reply letter to goods damage

> July 28
>
> Dear Mr. David,
>
> Thank you for your letter of July 27, in which you complained to us that parts of our goods were in a damaged condition. Now we are writing to offer you our proposals for settling this matter.
>
> Upon receipt of your letter, we gave this matter our immediate attention, studied your survey report carefully and conducted an investigation. We found it was indeed caused by our improper packing. Therefore we would like to accept your advice to reduce the price to 50%.
>
> We apologize once again for any inconvenience, and we hope this matter will not influence our future cooperation. Looking forward to your larger order.
>
> Sincerely yours,
> Miss Emma

Sample 2: Reply letter to poor quality

January 3

Dear Miss Shelly,

  We have received your letter dated May 2, informing us of the problems of electronic dictionary. We would like to express our deep regret about this matter, and thank you for telling it to us.

  We are very concerned about it and asked our technician to look into the dictionary carefully at once. It has been found that this matter is resulting from defective design. To this problem, we offer the solution that we either change it for another model or give you a complete refund for it. Again, we apologize for the inconvenience caused by us, and we hope the solution will satisfy you.

  We are looking forward to receiving your reply.

Yours faithfully,
Mr. Hunter
Market Manager

Sample 3: Reply letter to wrong delivery

Dear Johnson Black,

  Thank you for your letter of May 13 regarding your Order No.26.

  We are sorry to learn that there was a wrong delivery in your order. We are now sending consignment to you by air. It should reach you within a week. And the necessary documentation will be sent separately. Please hold the goods which were wrongly shipped for collection.

  We offer our sincere apologies for our mistake. Should you have any further problems, please do not hesitate to contact us immediately.

Truly yours,
Mr. Wang

Sample 4: Reply letter to short delivery

February 7

Dear Mr. Charlie,

  Thank you for your e-mail of February 6 regarding your order of January 25. We understand that this is difficult for you.

  We have investigated the situation and found that you ordered 1,000 mini fans. Please see the attached order form. Our dispatch office, therefore, sent 1,000.

If you need the remaining goods urgently, the balance of 100 fans can be dispatched today by express courier to you and would arrive by Thursday, February 14.

Please tell me if you would like to order these fans. We look forward to receiving your exact answers soon.

Yours sincerely,
Ms. Yang
Sales Manager

Sample Structure

1. Letterhead (if necessary)
2. Date
3. Inside name and address (if necessary)
4. Salutation
5. Body
6. Complimentary close
7. Signature
8. Job title (if necessary)
9. Company, organization (if necessary)
10. Contact way (if necessary)
11. Enclosures (if necessary)

Body Structure

The body usually consists of the following three parts.

1. Opening
2. Middle
3. Closing

Body Analysis

1. Opening: To express your thanks for the incoming letter and state the purpose for writing.

> Thank you for your letter of July 27, in which you complained to us that parts of our goods were in a damaged condition. Now we are writing to offer you our proposals for settling this matter.

2. Middle: To state the reasons causing the problem or error and provide the solution to the problem or error.

> Upon receipt of your letter, we gave this matter our immediate attention, studied your survey report carefully and conducted an investigation. We found it was indeed caused by our improper packing. Therefore we would like to accept your advice to reduce the price to 50%.

3. Closing: To express your apology again as well as your wishes or expectations.

> We apologize once again for any inconvenience, and we hope this matter will not influence our future cooperation. Looking forward to your larger order.

Writing Tips

1. Express your thanks and concern about the problem.
2. Clearly explain the reasons causing the problem.
3. Provide the solution to the problem.
4. Express your apology again and best wishes.
5. Write your letter with a friendly and complimentary tone, and avoid writing an angry, sarcastic, or threatening letter which will be not helpful in resolving problems.
6. Make your letter brief and to the point.
7. Type your letter if possible.
8. Keep a copy of the letter for your records.

Useful Expressions

1. We have received your e-mail of July 4 in which you make a complaint about broken genuine leather wallets.
我们已收到您7月4日关于真皮钱包破损的投诉邮件。
2. I am referring to your letter of October 10 regarding the poor quality of our products.
现就您10月10日来函提及的关于我方产品质量差的问题做出回复。
3. We feel terribly sorry to hear that you have lost USD 20,000 as a result of our delay in delivery.
我们非常抱歉,由于我方交货延误,贵方损失了两万美元。

4. With reference to your complaint letter of July 10, we express our deepest regret over the unfortunate incident.

关于贵方7月10日的投诉信,我们对发生的不幸事件深表遗憾。

5. Upon receipt of your complaint letter, we immediately made a thorough investigation on the matter.

收到贵方投诉信后,我们立即对此事进行了彻底调查。

6. We looked into the matter after receiving your letter, and found that your claim is perfectly justified.

收到贵方来信后,我们对此事进行了调查,认为贵方的要求是完全合理的。

7. Having checked with our suppliers, it is very clear that they mistakenly sent us a consignment of faulty goods.

经过向本公司的供应商核实,很明显他们将一批有瑕疵的货物错发给了本公司。

8. We find that the mistake is arising in confusing the order numbers, and two cartons for another order are sent to you.

我们发现是订单号混淆造成的错误,把另一个订单中的两箱货寄给了贵方。

9. We regret to inform you that we cannot give you a refund because it is not our fault.

我们很遗憾地通知您:不是我方的错,故不能为您退款。

10. The evidence you provided is not sufficient, so we can not make compensation for the claim that you entertain.

贵方提供的证据不充分,所以我方不能按贵方提出的条件做出赔偿。

11. It is not our fault because the goods were shipped in perfect condition as shown by the clean B/L enclosed.

这不是我方的过错,因为所附的清洁提单显示货物在装运时完好无损。

12. We advise you to file a claim against the shipping company, and we can facilitate you to deal with it if needed.

我们建议贵方向船运公司提出索赔,如有需要,我们可以协助贵方处理。

13. We shall remit to you an amount of 3,000 dollars by T/T in compensation for the loss incurred.

我方将通过电汇的方式向贵方汇3,000美元,赔偿由此造成的损失。

14. We offer the solution that we either change it for another computer or give you a complete refund for it.

我们提供的解决方案是:要么更换一台电脑,要么全额退款。

15. We are planning to rearrange to dispatch five new mountain bikes to replace the damaged ones within two days.

我们正计划在两天内重新安排发出五辆新的山地车来替换那些损坏的车辆。

16. We are ready to allow you 40% discount of the invoice value if you would like to accept the defective goods.

如果贵方愿意接受这批质量有瑕疵的货物,我们准备给予贵方发票金额40%的折扣。

17. We shall do everything we can in the future to ensure that something like that will not happen again.

今后我们将尽一切努力确保类似的事情不再发生。

18. We would like to extend you our deep apology for the inconvenience occurred to you.

由此为您造成的不便,我们深表歉意。

19. We apologize for the inconvenience caused by us, and we hope the solution we offer will satisfy you.

由此为您造成的不便,我们深表歉意,并希望我方提出的解决方案能让您满意。

20. We hope this unfortunate incident will not adversely affect our future business cooperation.

我们希望这一不幸事件不会影响我们今后的商务合作。

Task Solving

After studying what has been presented above, you may know how to compose a reply letter to complaint successfully.

Consolidation Exercise

1. Please fill in the blanks according to the initial letter.

Dear Mr. Colin,

Thank you for your letter of May 20, in (1) w_____ you informed us of the (2) s_____ weight of 9,000 kg of wheat. We would like to express our deep regret about this (3) m_____ .

We have (4) c_____ with our warehouse and (5) d_____ that this consignment was not completely packed as (6) r_____ . This was due to the negligence of our warehouse staff.

We are most concerned to (7) m_____ our long-standing trading relationship. We therefore (8) e_____ a check of 2,000 dollars as a (9) c_____ for your loss caused by us.

We hope that this incident will not (10) a_____ our future business relations.

Yours faithfully,

Miss Doris

2. Please translate the English underlined into Chinese.

Dear Mr. Li,

Thank you for your kind and objective feedback about our service. I am terribly sorry to hear that you experienced some trouble during your stay at our hotel and (1) <u>I would like to sincerely apologize to you on behalf of the hotel.</u>

After carefully reading your letter, I will address the issues you raised. Regarding the breakfast, we apologize if it was not up to your expectations. We understand that (2) <u>a variety of options would ensure you a satisfying start every day.</u> (3) <u>I can assure you that we will take your feedback seriously</u> and we will be working to improve our breakfast offerings.

As for the swimming pool closing at 9:00 p.m., we apologize for any discomfort occurred to you. We recognize that this time may not be convenient for all guests, and (4) <u>we will look into extending the swimming pool hours</u> to better accommodate our guests' needs and preferences.

Once again, I would like to express my sincere apologies for any inconvenience you may have experienced during your stay. We value your feedback and (5) <u>we are committed to making necessary improvements</u> to ensure that we meet and exceed your expectations. We look forward to welcoming you back to Sun Five Star Hotel next time and experiencing a wonderful stay here.

Sincerely yours,
John Wang
Customer Service Manager
Sun Five Star Hotel

3. Please translate the Chinese in the brackets into English.

Dear Miss Donna,

_____(我们收到了贵公司5月15日的来信，对此表示感谢), in which you mentioned that there was something wrong with the phones you ordered online from our company.

We examined it carefully as soon as we received your letter and regretted to find that _____(损毁的确是由包装不慎造成的). Considering the inconvenience it brought for you, _____(我们决定用新手机更换损毁的手机), and we will send them to you immediately. For the the phone battery life, it could be due to application software. If possible, _____(建议您卸载一些应用程序) or background tasks that may be consuming battery juice, which could be affecting the battery life. Furthermore, if the problem persists, we are willing to provide additional assistance and solutions.

> Anyway, we take full responsibility for all expenses incurred.
> We apologize once again for any inconvenience, and _____
> _____ (我们希望所提供的解决方案能使贵方满意) and everything will go well.
>
> Sincerely yours,
Mr. Nelson
Customer Service Center
Double E-commerce Company

Writing Practice

Directions: Suppose you are Miss Alisa, the sales manager of Perth Woolen Product Company. Yesterday you received a complaint letter from Miss Judy Li, one of your customers, in which she complained that there were 200 scarves with holes in them. Now you are writing a reply letter to settle this problem.

Module 5 Writing for Business Report and Proposal

Task 1 Business Report

 Learning Objectives

- Learn about the definition, function and types of business report.
- Be familiar with the structure, content and format of business report.
- Master the useful expressions such as words, phrases and sentences for business report.
- Be able to skillfully compose a correct business report in the real business situation.

 Task Situation

Recently, Mr. Stephen finds that more and more staff are late for work and some of them are frequently late. In order to find the reasons and address this problem, today (July 12) he requests Mabel to write an investigation report on staff's lateness. It includes an introduction of the general situation, reasons for lateness, and solutions to this issue.

Supposing you are Mabel, how do you finish the task assigned to you?

 Questions

- What basic contents are included in a business report?
- How are the structure and format of a business report?
- What points should we pay attention to when composing a business report?

 Theory Background

A business report is a highly specialized document that is presented to the supervisor of department or company. It often describes and analyzes the information or data collected. Then recommendations are presented to the decision-makers. A business report can provide decision-makers with new working ideas or provide reference for their next decision.

Business report plays a crucial role in business practice as most major decisions are based on it. And it is widely used in fields such as finance, accounting, management, marketing, investment, trade, and audit.

A business report is organized in a concise way and a standard format by using clearly defined sections, which tells readers why and how you did it, and what you have done and found.

According to the degree of formality, business report can be divided into two types: formal report and informal report.

According to the degree of length, business report can be divided into two types: long business report and short business report.

According to its style, business report can be divided into three types: memo format, letter format and pre-printed format.

According to its content, business report can be divided into various types, such as sales report, budget report, production report, finance report, adjustment report, accident report, etc.

According to its function, business report can be divided into various types, such as investigation report, feasibility report, progress report, trip report, etc.

According to the division of time, business report can be divided into various types, such as daily report, weekly report, monthly report, quarterly report, annual report, etc.

 Sample Study

Sample 1: Investigation report in formal format

Investigation Report on Glasses Product Market Share

Date: May 14

Reported by: Louise, Sales Manager

Terms of Reference

Upon request of General Manager, I am submitting the following investigation report on the market share in glasses products. This report aims to find out the reasons for losing market share and presents solutions to this problem.

Procedure

From March 12 till May 12 of this year, we did questionnaires online and interviewed our customers by telephone to discover the reasons behind it.

Finding

According to the results drawn from the investigation above, we get the following findings.

1. 46% of customers think that our products are outdated in style.

2. 53% of customers say that they do not have a big choice for our products.

---

3. 44% of customers hold the view that our products are too high in price.

4. 60% of customers find that our products are lack of technological innovation.

Conclusion

Based on the findings above, it can be concluded that some effective measures should be taken to enhance our product market share.

Recommendation

With reference to the facts stated above, we put forward the following recommendations.

1. We must develop more new-style products to attract more customers.

2. We should widen our product ranges to increase customers' choice.

3. We can adopt promotional strategies such as cash discounts, and special offers.

4. We may increase research and development funding to stay competitive.

Sample 2: Feasibility report in informal format

Feasibility Report on Buying Stocks of AAA Car Company

This report is to describe the current situation of AAA Car Company and to discuss whether we should buy stocks from that company.

Several investigations were carried out prior to this report and much information has been found out about AAA Car Company. According to the research, AAA Car Company is doing fine recently and has had a steady rise in profits five years in a row. The stock price of it got doubled last year after its taking over two rivals, which added to its categories of products.

Recently they shuffled management, and a famous person with fifteen years of management experience in that industry is appointed as the chairman of the company. As a result, the company is operating faster than ever before. What's more, the mini car industry is seeing a steady growth in demand and profits are huge, therefore, the stock price is sure to grow in the future. A series of up-to-date statistics show that the company runs very smoothly and has very strong profitability, which is good for its stock market.

With all the information and data listed, I believe buying stocks from the company can bring us huge profits in the future. I think it maybe more appropriate to start the purchasing of stocks right now as its present stock price is relatively low.

Sample 3: Progress report in letter format

Progress Report on Renovation of Bookstore

May 30

Dear Mr. Clark,

  The renovation of the bookstore is moving on schedule and is within the budget. The cost of paint is higher than our original estimate because we chose a new product that doesn't contain harmful chemicals and releases no odor; but the air-conditioners' price has gone down a great deal, offsetting the increase in spending on paint. We expect to complete the project without exceeding the budget.

Costs

  The materials used so far have cost RMB 5,000, and the labour costs are RMB 10,000. Our estimate for the remaining project is RMB 13,000, RMB 5,000 going to the costs of materials and RMB 8,000 to the labor costs.

Work Completed

  By May 29, we had painted the walls, changed the windows and doors, and installed air-conditioners. We had planted tree and grass around the bookstore. The replacement of lights and ventilators are in the preliminary stages.

Work to Be Completed

  We have scheduled the replacement of illuminations and ventilators to take place from June 1 to 3 and the installation of flooring from June 10 to 20.

  We see no difficulty in completing the project by the scheduled date of July 1.

Yours sincerely,
Dick Smith

Sample 4: Trip report in memo format

Trip Report on Two Factories in Texas from March 25 to 28

To: John Wilson, General Manager

From: Jim Dyer, Production Manager

Date: September 21

Subject: Trip Report on Two Factories in Texas from March 25 to 28

Introduction

  From March 25 to 28, I visited two of our factories in Texas and discussed with the directors about the problems our factories are facing.

Finding

We saw places where incidents might occur. The directors agreed that they had to do something about them. There were a lot of hidden dangers.

1. A number of fire extinguishers were out of date;
2. The water pressure was too low;
3. Chemicals were left near cotton piles and plastic.

Recommendation

We think some measures need to be taken immediately.

Firstly, draft a crisis plan and make it publicized throughout the factories.

Secondly, keep dangerous materials in the special storage away from the workshops.

Sample Structure

1. Head/Title
2. Date
3. Reporter
4. Introduction/Terms of reference
5. Procedure/Proceeding/Methodology
6. Finding
7. Conclusion
8. Recommendation/Suggestion/Proposal

Or:

1. Head/Title
2. Date
3. Reporter
4. Introduction (including Terms of reference, Procedure/Proceeding/Methodology)
5. Finding (including Conclusion)
6. Recommendation/Suggestion/Proposal

Structure Analysis

1. Head/Title: To state the subject matter of report; it usually writes as follows.

Report; Investigation Report on Glasses Product Market Share; REPORT ON WASTE IN COMPANY

2. Date: To state when the report is written.

Date: May 14

3. Reporter: To state by whom the report is written.

> Reported by: Louise, Sales Manager

4. Introduction/Terms of reference: To explain the background information such as the reasons and purpose for writing, and problems to be discussed.

> Upon request of General Manager, I am submitting the following investigation report on market share in glasses products. This report aims to find out the reasons for market share loss and present solutions to this problem.

5. Procedure/Proceeding/Methodology: To state the proceeding or methodology used for collecting data and facts for the report.

> From March 12 till May 12 of this year, we did questionnaires online and interviewed our customers by telephone to discover the reasons behind it.

6. Finding: To describe what has been found in the report or discovered about the problems.

> According to the results drawn from the investigation above, we get the following findings.
> 1. 46% of customers think that our products are outdated in style.
> 2. 53% of customers say that they do not have a big choice for our products.
> 3. 44% of customers hold the view that our products are too high in price.
> 4. 60% of customers find that our products are lack of technological innovation.

7. Conclusion: To state the implications inferred from the findings.

> Based on the findings above, it can be concluded that some effective measures should be taken to enhance our product share.

8. Recommendation/Suggestion/Proposal: To provide suggestions or proposals to solve the problem.

> With reference to the facts stated above, we put forward the following recommendations.
> 1. We must develop more new-style products to attract more customers.
> 2. We should widen our product ranges to increase customers' choice.
> 3. We can adopt promotional strategies such as cash discounts, and special offers.
> 4. We may increase research and development funding to stay competitive.

Writing Tips

1. Be clear in your mind what the purpose is and who are the readers of your report.

2. State clearly the method of gathering information for the report such as through research, interviews, and questionnaires.

3. Describe what you have found from the facts and data.

4. Draw your conclusions from the findings and propose your recommendations to the problem.

5. Select the appropriate format for the report.

6. Choose a proper tone. An effective tone should be:

(1) Objective: eliminate personal feelings and prejudice towards facts observed;

(2) Definite: stick to facts, use figures, and be confident;

(3) Positive: be sure of what you want to let your readers know;

(4) Upward: be upward when you write to your supervisor;

(5) Downward: be downward when you write to your subordinate.

7. Adopt the appropriate style. To make your report in good shape, the following are important:

(1) Be simple and varied in style;

(2) Use a mixture of long and short sentences;

(3) Divide long report by titling different parts;

(4) Use figures, tables, charts, and photos to add visual effect and enhance readability;

(5) Use present tense in stating facts and figures;

(6) Be accurate in reference.

Useful Expressions

1. Terms of reference

(1) As is requested by/Upon request of General Manager, I am submitting/presenting the following report about investment.

按总经理的要求,现提供以下关于投资的报告。

(2) As you requested on July 5, I am presenting the following report on staff's service attitude.

按您7月5日的要求,现呈交以下关于员工服务态度的报告。

(3) The following is the feasibility report you requested on November 18.

下面是您11月18日要求的可行性报告。

(4) HR Manager asked me to write a report on the feasibility of introducing automatic office system.

人事部经理要求我写一份关于引进自动化办公系统的可行性报告。

(5) The purpose/aim/objective of this report is to investigate/examine/evaluate/assess/study/recommend/analyze/estimate/summarize our training system of company for staff.

本报告的目的是调查/考察/评价/评估/研究/建议/分析/估计/总结我们公司的员工培训体系。

(6) This report/proposal/investigation aims/sets out/serves/tries/intends to discover the reasons for the decrease in sales volume.

本报告/建议/调查的目的是发现销售量下降的原因。

(7) Here is the report concerning the budget next year.

下面是关于明年预算的报告。

2. Procedure/Proceeding/Methodology

(1) Eighty questionnaires were sent to all staff on November 10, fifty of whom are male and thirty female.

11月10日向员工发放了80份调查问卷,其中50名男员工,30名女员工。

(2) Thirty-five questionnaire about the transport methods and reasons for lateness were sent to all staff on September 21.

9月21日,就交通工具及迟到原因向全体员工发放了35份调查问卷。

(3) From December 12 last year till January 12 this year, we have been doing an investigation on our glasses product market share.

从去年12月12日至今年1月12日,我们就眼镜产品市场份额做了调查。

(4) We conducted this investigation by on-line surveys and through telephone interviews with our regular customers to find the reasons for the problems.

为了找到问题背后的原因,我们通过网络调查和电话访谈对我们的老客户进行了调查。

(5) Questionnaires were completed by 80 employees from 4 departments and 10 of the respondents were interviewed.

4个部门的80名员工填写了问卷,其中10人接受了访谈。

(6) We commissioned an independent research firm to interview our customers to understand how they like our products.

我们委托一家独立调查公司采访我们的客户,以了解他们对我们产品的看法。

3. Finding

(1) The main findings from the survey are outlined below.

调查的主要发现如下。

(2) The following points summarize our key findings.

下面几点就是我们的主要发现。

(3) According to the data drawn from questionnaire/survey/interview, the findings are as follows.

根据问卷调查/调查/访谈得出的数据,发现如下。

(4) The recent investigation/survey shows that our products are more and more popular with consumers.

最近的调查表明,我们的产品越来越受消费者的欢迎。

(5) The table/chart/statistics below tells us there is a steady increase in the number of customers.

下面的表格/图表/统计数字表明客户的数量在稳步增加。

(6) As is shown in the chart above, we find/learn that jobless rate falls to 4.3% in December from 5.5% in November.

如上图所示,我们发现/了解到失业率从11月份的5.5%下降到12月的4.3%。

(7) It was found/discovered that most business people are very confident about the prospects of the world economy.

我们发现,绝大多数商务人士对世界经济前景充满信心。

(8) Many staff members expressed the view that good company's image is helpful for promoting products.

很多员工表达了这个观点:良好的公司形象有助于产品销售。

(9) According to the recent research/investigation, we find/realize that the waste phenomena are very serious.

根据最近的研究/调查,我们发现/意识到浪费现象非常严重。

(10) From the chart shown below, we find that it is very necessary to improve our salespersons' English proficiency.

如下表所示,我们发现很有必要提高销售人员的英语水平。

(11) The chart above is showing that we should increase the additional budget for public relations department in the coming year.

上图表明,我们应该增加公共关系部门明年的预算外经费。

(12) We have done a survey showing that the degree of customers' satisfaction is increasing.

我们做过调研,发现客户的满意度越来越高。

4. Conclusion

(1) With reference to the findings above, we can get the following conclusions.

根据上述发现,我们可以得出如下结论。

(2) According to the findings above, the following conclusions can be made/got.

根据上述发现,我们可以得出如下结论。

(3) Based on the findings above, we can summarize that marketing department urgently needs to recruit new members.

基于上述发现,我们得出结论:市场部急需招聘新成员。

(4) From the table shown above, it can be concluded that we should launch our new products in American market as soon as possible.

如上表所示,我们得出结论:应该尽快在美国市场投放我们的新产品。

(5) Therefore, it can be generalized that we will have to take on more expense if we provide 24-hour online service.

因此,我们的结论是,如果提供24小时在线服务,我们将不得不承担更多的费用。

(6) Our conclusions are that workers' salaries should be raised.

我们的结论是,应提高工人的工资。

5. Recommendation/Suggestion/Proposal

(1) The following are our recommendations.

下面是我们的建议。

(2) Based on the conclusion/analysis/results above, we can put forward the following advice.

基于上述结论/分析/结果,我们提出如下建议。

(3) With reference to the facts stated above, the following suggestions can be made.

根据上述事实,我们建议如下。

(4) On the basis of the analysis above, we recommend that advertising in traditional media should be stopped at once.

根据上述分析,我们建议必须立即停止在传统媒体上投放广告。

(5) We would strongly recommend/suggest that the quality of after-sales service should be improved.

我们强烈建议必须提高售后服务的质量。

(6) It is suggested/proposed/recommended that all staff should exercise fire drill at least twice a year.

我们建议全体员工一年最少应进行两次消防技能演练。

(7) It would be/is advisable to update product information on our online shop every day.

建议每天更新我们网店的产品信息。

(8) It is advised/proposed/suggested to enhance salespersons' service awareness.

建议提高销售人员的服务意识。

Task Solving

After studying what has been presented above, you may know how to compose a business report successfully.

商务英语写作

 Consolidation Exercise

1. Please fill in the blanks according to the initial letter.

Feasibility Report on In-house Training Courses

Date: September 21

Reported by: Miss Betty

Terms of Reference

As (1) r_____ by HR Director, Mr. Bernard, the (2) p_____ of this report is to examine the feasibility of holding in-house training courses.

Methodology

External training providers are (3) c_____. Internal and external training costs are compared. Questionnaires were (4) c_____ by 80 employees from 4 departments and 10 of the respondents were (5) i_____.

Finding

The key findings from the survey are (6) o_____ below.

1. After a careful comparison, it can be calculated that in-house training will reduce the cost by 26%, compared with external training.

2. 65% of staff think that internal training can be designed to (7) s_____ the specific needs of the organization, and therefore it will benefit the company as a whole.

3. Those who have filled questionnaires hold the (8) v_____ that they are more likely to participate in training courses if they are held in-house.

Conclusion

Based on the (9) a_____ of the investigation above, the following conclusions can be (10) d_____:

1. Considerable savings will be made if in-house training is held.

2. 93% of employees feel that they are more likely to participate in in-house training.

Recommendation

According to the findings above, it is feasible to hold an in-house training.

---

2. Please translate the English underlined into Chinese.

To: Michael, General Manager

From: Bill, Marketing Manager

Date: September 9

An Investigation on Slimming-down of the Head Office

Introduction

From March to June, with the instruction of the board, we made a slimming-down of the head office in Seattle. (1) The report is on matter of the slimming-down and our advice for future alike action.

Findings

(2) A slow market have led to 3 overseas plants and 1 home branch closed since last July, so redundancy occurred in the head office in Seattle, as the management team seemed too big for the shrunken production team.

But layoffs would result in a dispute with the Union. After several attempts of negotiation, a solution was made in September that the redundancies were to be rearranged in different ways so that (3) the employees' pensions and developments could be taken into broadest consideration.

Solution

First, those(seven) aged above 55 were retired with a sum of pension (4,600 dollars per year in the company's service) paid as compensation.

Second, (4) those aged between 45 and 54 were sent to take a 5-week training course of new skills. After finishing the course, a test was made and the first 24 (35 all together took the test) were sent to plants to strengthen the management. The remaining 11 quit the job with three months salary.

Conclusion

The slimming-down cost time and money, but was worthwhile. With the help of the Union, it was done without too much conflict. It also made staff realize that regular training courses are very important and they are now very eager to take some part-time courses.

Recommendation

(5) Such decision concerning the staff's interest needs consultation with the Union beforehand.

3. Please translate the Chinese in the brackets into English.

To: Miss Tania
From: Cindy Wu
Date: April 12
Subject: An Investigation Report on Staff's Job Satisfaction

Terms of Reference

In response to your request, _____
_____(报告的目的是分析员工的职业满意度) according to the collected questionnaires.

Methodology

A questionnaire survey was conducted to learn about the job satisfaction in our company. _____(58位员工按时交回了他们的调查问卷). In order to gain more factual figures, the employees were required to fill it anonymously.

Finding

According to the statistics, we get the following findings.

1. Most of the employees in total are content with their work.

2. It is found that the female staff (75%) are more satisfied with their present job than the male staff (63%).

3. _____(数据显示,薪水与幸福感没有相关性). 87% of younger people, aged 20 to 30, with lower payment, expresses their approval.

4. Meanwhile, 52% of the staff, aged 30 to 40, and 61%, aged 40 to 50, are more pessimistic.

However, some employees are not satisfied with the present situation and the reasons for dissatisfaction mentioned are as follows.

1. Little chance to get promoted or training.

2. Uncomfortable working environment.

3. Poor welfare system.

Conclusion

_____(基于上述发现,我们可以得出结论) that most people in our company look at their present job optimistically, but there is still space for our company to make some progress.

Recommendation

_____(建议调整晋升政策和福利制度) to stimulate staff to be more enthusiastic about their work.

Writing Practice

Directions: Suppose you are Cindy Li, a clerk in HR Department of America Nelson Shoes Company. Mr. Smith, your HR manager, asks you to write a report on proposing an incentive scheme, possibly financial, to those staff members who provide ideas for saving cost or ways of improving work efficiency.

Task 2 Business Proposal

 Learning Objectives

• Learn about the definition, function and types of business proposal.
• Be familiar with the structure, content and format of business proposal.
• Master the useful expressions such as words, phrases and sentences for business proposal.
• Be able to skillfully compose a correct business proposal in the real business situation.

 Task Situation

Recently Mr. Stephen receives some staff's complaints about the management that as the number of staff in your office has trebled over the past two years, the staff canteen gets uncomfortably overcrowded during the lunch break between 12:00 and 13:00. Several suggestions for overcoming the problems have been put forward by members of staff, such as enlarging the canteen, staggering the break instead of everybody having lunch at the same time. Therefore he requires Mable to write a proposal for solving this problem.

Supposing you are Mabel, how do you finish the task assigned to you?

 Questions

• What basic contents are included in a business proposal?
• How are the structure and format of a business proposal?
• What points should we pay attention to when composing a business proposal?

 Theory Background

A business proposal is a persuasive offer to solve problems, provide service, or sell products. It is an evaluation of a program or a strategy-to-be, based on its close study and a full consideration on its advantages and disadvantages of the future effect.

A business proposal is written to help decision-makers choose between two or more courses of action. It should assess whether the plan is practical in terms of available technology, finances, labor and other resources, and it also justifies why the other potential solutions might not be viable.

According to the degree of formality, business proposal can be divided into formal proposal and informal proposal.

According to its style, business proposal can be divided into memo format proposal, letter format proposal and pre-printed format proposal.

According to its function, business proposal can be divided into various types, such as proposal for investment, proposal for incentive system, proposal for changing working hour, proposal for opening a new branch, etc.

According to the situation used in, business proposal can be divided into internal business proposal and external business proposal.

Sample Study

Sample 1: Proposal for opening a nursery (formal format)

> Date: July 6
>
> Written by: Johnson, Marketing Manager
>
> **Introduction**
>
> As Mr. Scott requested, I am presenting this proposal with the aim to open a nursery at our shopping center.
>
> **Proceedings**
>
> In order to do this, the following steps have been taken.
>
> 1. I obtain a decline of customers with young children.
>
> 2. I discuss this issue with several customers who bring children to our shopping center.
>
> 3. I investigate the experience of other shopping centers that already have a nursery.
>
> **Findings**
>
> 1. 15% of our customers whom I interview have at least one child under the age of three.
>
> 2. 80% of our customers say that they will give consideration if there is a nursery.
>
> **Conclusion**
>
> The nursery will be popular with our customers if it is safe and clean with qualified keepers and reasonable costs.
>
> **Recommendation**
>
> After a detailed analysis, it is suggested to open a nursery in our shopping center.

Sample 2: Proposal for investment in BBO Chemicals and LIO Chemicals (informal format)

> Last week we visited the Investment Consultant Agency of New York to see whether we could have an cooperation with BBO Chemicals or LIO Chemicals. This proposal aims to assess which company we should invest in.

> The information was mainly achieved by discussing with the senior investment consultant Mr. Charlie Turner and observing personally their annual reports last year for shareholders.
>
> We found the turnover of BBO Chemicals increased by approximately 27.5%, and total export figures rose by at least 5%. Moreover, restructuring may expect growth in the northwest market and its advanced production line suggests opportunities for increasing profits. However, the results of LIO Chemicals were disappointing, with turnover and profit both falling dramatically. Besides, the company currently has a problem that many employees are leaving.
>
> Any investment in LIO Chemicals would involve a risk. BBO Chemicals, on the other hand, despite its present inefficiency, looks feasible and profitable, and it shows a high possibility for success and has a definite potential for further growth.
>
> Thus, we would recommend investment in BBO Chemicals.

Sample 3: Proposal for improving company rules and regulations (memo format)

> ### A proposal for improving company rules and regulations
>
> To: Kenneth Brown
>
> From: Julian White
>
> ### Introduction
>
> This proposal aims to analyse the current situation of the implementation of current company rules and give recommendation for improvement.
>
> ### Findings
>
> The current rules and regulations are operating smoothly and everything is in order. Everything can be regulated in the office and staffs are all well acquainted with them. However, there seems to be some problems in execution, and a few of the rules and regulations seem to be conflict with each other. A recent survey about the staff and their routine jobs found that some rules and regulations are standing in the way of their daily work and others can't keep up with the developing situation.
>
> ### Conclusions
>
> To sum up, it is urgent that the current rules and regulations be improved as soon as possible.
>
> ### Recommendations
>
> In order to make our work run more smoothly and the rules and regulations more standardized, I would like to make the following recommendations.

1. The regulations about punching twice at noon, before and after 12:30 separately should be revised to punch once at noon, which could avoid some unnecessary mistakes.

2. Methods of performance evaluation should be more specific and clear, so that employees can know exactly how to behave and what they can or cannot do.

Sample 4: Proposal for improving product sales (letter format)

Dear Mr. Mark,

This proposal has been prepared to recommend ways of improving sales of one of our products. All the figures are collected from the statistical data and questionnaires to the customers of and by the sales department.

After a thorough investigation to the customers and an elaborate analysis to the figures, we found that the current problems can be traced down to the following reasons. First, the name of the product is not very attractive and most customers who saw it didn't associate it with any kind of food. Second, the color of the packages are not fresh enough to attract children, who are easily appealed by more colorful packages. Third, the products are displayed in the higher rack of the shelves in the supermarket, so children can't see them easily.

As a result, I strongly recommend that some measures be taken to improve sales and attract more customers. First, the name of the product should be changed, so customers can know what it is when they see it. Second, the package of the product should be designed to be more attractive. Third, the products should be displayed in the bottom of the shelves. The only disadvantage we can envisage is that some of the customers have begun to know the products well and the changing of name and colors will disturb them from buying them.

However, in view of the long-term development, I recommend that the above measures be taken to attract more customers and create more profits.

Yous sincerely,
Frank Johnson

Sample Structure

1. Head/Title
2. Date (if necessary)
3. Writer (if necessary)
4. Introduction/Terms of reference
5. Procedures/Proceedings/Methodology
6. Findings
7. Conclusions
8. Recommendations/Suggestions/Proposals

Structure Analysis

1. Head/Title: Just write the usual title "A proposal for..." either in small letters or in capital ones.

> A Proposal
> A Proposal for Opening a Nursery
> A PROPOSAL FOR OPENING A NURSERY

2. Date: To state when the proposal is written.

> Date: July 6

3. Writer: To state by whom the proposal is written.

> Reported by: Johnson, Marketing Manager

4. Introduction/Terms of reference: To explain the background information such as the reasons and purposes for writing, and problems to be discussed.

> As Mr. Scott requested, I am presenting this report with the aim to investigate the opening of a nursery at our shopping center.

5. Procedures/Proceedings/Methodology: To explain the proceedings or methodology used for collecting data and facts for the proposal.

> In order to do this, the following steps have been taken.
> 1. I obtain a decline of customers with young children.
> 2. I discuss this issue with several customers who bring children to our shopping center.
> 3. I investigate the experience of other shopping centers that already have a nursery.

6. Findings: To present what has been found.

> * 15% of our customers whom I interview have at least one child under the age of three.
> * 80% of our customers say that they will give consideration if there is a nursery.

7. Conclusions: To state the implications inferred from the findings.

> The nursery will be popular with our customers if it is safe and clean with qualified keepers and reasonable costs.

8. Recommendations/Suggestions/Proposals: To provide suggestions for the target readers.

> After a detailed analysis, it is suggested to open a nursery in our shopping center.

 Writing Tips

1. Strictly follow the format and use titles, headings, subheadings, etc.
2. Crucial information and data should be included in the content.
3. Do not include any irrelevant specifics.
4. Present information in a way that readers can understand quickly.
5. Sum up its main idea in one sentence and use this as your heading.
6. The language should be rich in terms of patterns and words.
7. Make sure that the tense and voice is correctly employed.
8. Proofread the report and check spelling, grammar, etc.

 Useful Expressions

1. Introduction/Terms of reference

(1) As you requested the other day, I am presenting the following report on staff's performance of our company's employees.

按您前几天所要求的,现呈交以下关于公司员工绩效的报告。

(2) The finance manager instructed me to write a report on the feasibility of automated accounting processing.

财务部经理吩咐我写一份报告,内容关于账务自动化处理的可行性。

(3) This report/proposal/investigation aims to/sets out to discover the reasons for frequent delays in delivery of overseas goods.

本报告/建议/调查的目的是找出境外货物经常延迟交付的原因。

2. Procedures/Proceedings/Methodology

(1) We conducted a survey among randomly selected passers-by to collect information on the fashion styles this year.

我们在随机挑选的路人中进行了一项调查,收集人们对今年流行服装款式的意见。

(2) We conducted a month-long survey on the efficacy, price, and packaging of female cosmetics products designed for users aged 20 to 50.

我们就目标顾客为20岁至50岁女性的化妆品的功效、价格和包装情况做了为期一个月的调查。

(3) We invite five employees nominated by each department to participate in the sympo-

sium and conduct a written questionnaire survey.

我们邀请各部门推荐的5位员工参加座谈并进行书面的问卷调查。

3. Findings

(1) The key points of our investigation into the market share of our company's products are as follows.

我们对本公司产品的市场份额的调查要点如下。

(2) The popularity of our small electro-mechanical products in the East African market exceeds that of equivalent-sized cities in China by far.

我们的小机电产品在东非市场的受欢迎程度远超国内同等规模的城市。

(3) As shown in the pie chart, we found that the demand for purified water in cities is significantly lower than that for mineral water.

如饼状图所示,我们发现城市里纯净水的需求量远远小于矿泉水。

(4) The front desk layout of the company affects the impression of visiting customers on the company.

公司的前台布置影响前来拜访的客户对公司的印象。

(5) According to a random telephone survey, 80% of employees have a strong interest in learning local dialects.

根据电话随机调查结果,80%的员工对学习当地方言有浓厚的兴趣。

(6) We have done an in-depth survey showing that the majority of people are concerned about the increasing cost of living and the impact it has on their daily lives.

我们做了一项深入的调查,显示大多数人都担心生活成本的上涨及其对日常生活的影响。

4. Conclusions

(1) With reference to the research on the topic of salary, our conclusion is as follows: the average annual salary in the city is around RMB 50,000, but this varies depending on industry, location, and job type.

根据对薪酬主题的研究,我们的结论是:该市的平均年薪约为5万元人民币,但在不同行业、地点和工作类型方面,年薪有差别。

(2) Based on the findings above, we recommend implementing a targeted sales promotion strategy that offers discounts and incentives to customers who meet specific criteria.

根据上述调查结果,我们建议实施有针对性的促销策略,为符合特定标准的客户提供折扣和奖励。

(3) In conclusion, convenience stores that operate around the clock can fulfill nighttime shopping needs.

总之,全天候营业的便利店可以人们满足夜间购物的需求。

5. Recommendations

(1) In light of the conclusions mentioned, we deem it necessary to take into account the

crucial elements of price, quality, and popularity.

基于以上结论,我们认为价格、质量和受欢迎程度都是需要考虑的重要因素。

(2) After detailed and rigorous analysis, it is recommended to carry out moderate eco-friendly packaging of the product.

经过详细而严谨的分析,我们建议产品采用适度的环保包装。

(3) It is necessary to increase the efficiency of after-sales service and the number of personnel, which would help enhance the competitiveness of the automotive industry.

有必要提高售后服务的效率和人员数量,这将有助于增强汽车行业的竞争力。

(4) From any perspective, it is suggested that small and medium-sized enterprises tightly grasp the middle and low-income groups as an important way to achieve market success.

无论从哪个角度看,都建议中小企业紧紧抓住中低收入群体,这是它们在市场上获得成功的重要途径。

 Task Solving

After studying what has been presented above, you may know how to compose a business proposal successfully.

 Consolidation Exercise

1. Please fill in the blanks according to the initial letter.

Proposal on the Closure of One of the Factories

Introduction

The aim of this proposal is to analyse and (1) a_____ the reasons and effects of the closure of one of our factories and recommend further steps thenceforth.

Reasons for closure

In light of the (2) s_____ of reintegrating global resources, it is necessary for our company to close the factory in Jiangsu for the following reasons. The (3) u_____ of costs, including those of labor force and raw materials, mainly (4) c_____ to the closure, which gains 90% of the respondents in the survey who consider it is wise to close down the factory. Also, the increasingly fierce local (5) c_____ cannot be ignored when considering the closure of the factory in question.

Possible effects

As the production (6) c_____ of the local factory has seldom taken up the major market share, the closure will be more symbolic than real. As a result, it will not exert dramatic (7) n_____ effects on the rest of our company. However, the social influence of

---

206

the closure should not be (8) u_____ , that is, the large amount of workers who are to be made redundant might pose potential risks—the harmonious development of society.

Recommendations

It would be (9) a_____ for our company to transfer the manufacturing function to other lower-cost regions such as Southeast Asia. Meanwhile, it is (10) u_____ for our company to upgrade industries to face the challenge of globalization and industrial restructuring should be on the agenda.

2. Please translate the English underlined into Chinese.

Proposal for product advertisement

To: Mr. Black, Sales Director
From: Henry Brown, Salesman

Introduction

(1) <u>The sales of our VC juice last quarter is not very satisfying</u>, with net profits goes down by 1.5%. And it doesn't seem to be getting better this quarter, from April to June. On the contrary, our competitor's products are doing fine.

Observations

(2) <u>Extensive advertising is a key factor for our rivals' success</u>. While our company stopped advertisement and publicity last quarter, there was a significant decrease in sales. And some new rivals' entering the market surly intensified the competition. Therefore, I suggest that some advertisements be made to attract customers to publicize our products.

Recommendations

I hope the following measures can be taken to advertise products.

(3) <u>First, some posters should be made for sales promotion</u> as summer will be the best season for juice, so I think that posters of various juice products should be pasted and given out. That will cost us about 100 dollars.

(4) <u>Second, some more advertisement should be made on TV</u> to show the new taste and package of our products, and teenagers will like that very much. The ad should appear at 19:00 every day, three months in a row. That will cost us about 1,200 dollars.

Third, as most colleges surf the net nowadays, some interesting games and flashes advertising our products should be put on the internet. And more posters should be given out to internet bars. That will total to about 1,600 dollars.

Conclusion

With these advertisements and sales promotion, (5) <u>I'm sure our company can regain our leading position</u> in VC juice market.

3. Please translate the Chinese in the brackets into English.

Proposal on the Improvement of Intra-Company Communication

Introduction

_____(本建议旨在总结公司各部门之间沟通不畅所造成的问题) and suggest possible ways of improving the situation. The analysis is based on data collected by way of questionnaires dispatched among staff members of the various departments of our company.

Problems caused by poor communication between departments

First, inefficient information sharing among different departments. _____
_____(由于我们是一家IT公司，信息共享和升级对我们公司的发展至关重要).

Second, poor coordination among departments. Taking customer service as an example, due to the inefficient communication between departments, different departments present different information and even different attitudes to our customers. This will undoubtedly compromise our company's reputation.

Third, low staff morale. _____
___(由于各部门都有自己的工作要做，大家逐渐养成了只关心自己部门利益的习惯), and sometimes they even harm the benefits of other departments. All this will inevitably result in low staff morale.

Ways of improving communication between departments

First, _____(每周五下午召开周例会，各部门负责人参加).

Second, we can apply modern computer software—OA (Office Anywhere). The staff members can send each other e-mails or chat on OA.

Benefits of improved communication between departments

First, have more efficient information sharing, as well as better work efficiency.

Second, _____(对外人，例如我们的客户，采取统一的态度，以提升公司形象和影响力).

Third, boost staff morale, and achieve better performance of the company.

Writing Practice

Directions: Suppose you are are Miss Zhao, the secretary of General Manager of Sunrise Company. You have received some complaints that some computers don't work well and affect work efficiency. Therefore, you decide to write a proposal for changing the computers with problems and present the proposal to your general manager.

The main points are as follows.

(1) What problems exist in some computers.

(2) What are the consequences of the problems.

(3) What are your solutions to the problems.

Appendix

一、常见的英语写作微信公众号

(1) 英语写作菌
(2) 英语写作教学与研究
(3) 英文悦读

二、常见的英语写作学习网站

1. 新东方商务英语写作(http://yingyu.xdf.cn/list 1807_1.html)

新东方商务英语写作网站主要是为职场人士、商务英语专业学生及有志于提升商务英语写作能力的人设计的。通过系统学习,学习者可以掌握商务英语写作的基本技能、格式要求及写作技巧,准确地进行商务信函的写作,撰写高质量的商务报告、商务提案和商务合同,在商务环境中高效地进行书面沟通。网站内容覆盖商务英语写作的各个方面,从基础写作要点到高级写作技能逐步深入。通过模拟写作练习和案例分析,学习者能够在实践中提升写作能力。

2. 沪江英语BEC中级(http://www.hjenglish.com/beczhongji/beczjxiezuo/)

该网站是为学习者提升商务英语写作能力而设计的,致力于帮助学习者掌握BEC中级考试的写作要领,为学习者提供写作技巧、示例文章、模拟试题等学习资源;包含BEC中级考试写作格式的讲解,如书信、报告、议论文等不同文体的写作要求,提供高分范文和模板,供学习者参考和学习;提供备考BEC中级考试写作题的具体建议,如时间管理、题目分析、草稿规划等,通过模拟试题和练习,帮助学习者熟悉考试形式,提高应试能力。另外,网站上还有互动和交流模块,学习者可以相互交流,还能相互提供反馈,以提升写作水平。

3. 香港理工大学英语写作教学平台(http://www2.elc.polyu.edu.hk/CILL/writing.htm)

该网站详细介绍了商务英语写作类型、格式、资源、技巧、反馈、调整等方面的内容,能为学习者提供丰富而全面的写作指导。借助这些资源,学习者可以系统地提高自己的写作能力,满足学习和工作方面的需求。

4. Perfect Your English商务英语(http://www.perfectyourenglish.com/businessenglish/business-english.htm)

Perfect Your English商务英语网站为学习者提供了商务英语写作技巧、范文以及其他相关学习内容,列出了多种正式信函的样文,包括解雇信、终止业务关系信、询问信、任命信、辞职信、推荐信、参考信、请假信、祝贺信等。这些范文涵盖了商务英语写作的多个方面,为学习者提供了具有应用价值的参考意见。

5. 阿德莱德大学写作中心（https://www.adelaide.edu.au/writingcentre/resources/writing-resources#preparing-to-write）

阿德莱德大学写作中心是致力于提升学习者写作技能的综合性服务机构，能为学习者提供预约咨询、在线课程、写作资源和指南。为了使所有学习者都能获得全面的写作支持，阿德莱德大学写作中心在写作框架构思、资料收集、文章修改等各阶段为学习者提供帮助。

6. Varsity Tutors 写作（https://www.varsitytutors.com/englishteacher/writing.html）

该网站致力于帮助学生和教师提高写作技能，通过提供丰富的教学课程、工具和资源，以及个性化的教学方法，满足不同学生的学习需求。同时，该网站还强调创意写作和学术写作的重要性，鼓励学生发展独特的写作风格，并掌握学术写作规范。此外，通过写作工作坊、研讨会和优秀作品展示，该网站还能促进学生之间的交流和学习，在学生之间形成积极向上的写作学习氛围。

7. 英国国家统计局官方网站（www.ons.gov.uk/ons/index.html）

这是英国国家统计局（Office for National Statistics，ONS）的官方网站，有大量英国官方公布的就业、人口、经济、社会等多个领域的统计数据和分析报告，对学习者学习客观分析和图表描述类文章的写作很有帮助。

8. ProCon.org 网站（www.procon.org）

这是一个非营利性质的公益网站，专注于提供中立、全面的观点讨论内容，通过广泛的议题覆盖、实时的新闻更新、深入的法律政策讨论以及权威的数据支持，为学习者提供思考、交流和学习的空间。该网站通过提供对常见的、具有广泛争议话题的不同观点，培养学习者的批判性思维能力。在该网站，学习者几乎可以找到所有常见话题的正反方观点，比如枪支管控（gun control）、动物实验（animal testing）以及社交网络的好处与坏处（the pros and cons of social networking）等。学习者可以通过模仿来提升思维水平和写作能力。

9. WritingDEN（www2.actden.com/writ_den/tips/contents.htm）

该网站为学习者提供了一站式的写作提升指导，网站内容涵盖了句子、段落、论文等多个方面的写作技巧和提示，旨在帮助学习者更好地撰写文章，提高写作效率和质量。

10. 中华人民共和国商务部官方网站"分析报告"板块（http://www.mofcom.gov.cn/fxbg/index.html）

该板块主要发布了一系列关于中国商务和经济发展的重要报告，内容涵盖了对外投资合作、电子商务、服务贸易、数字贸易等多个领域，旨在为公众提供全面、权威、及时的中国商务和经济发展信息。学习者可以通过该板块了解权威的商务信息，分析并掌握商务报告的写作技巧。

三、常见的英语作文自动评分系统和网站

1. 批改网(http://www.pigai.org/)

批改网是智能批改英语作文的在线服务网站,它通过将学习者的英语作文和海量标准语料库进行对比分析,能在1.2秒内为英语作文给出分数、评语、按句纠错的批改反馈。该网站能有效帮助英语写作教师提高批改作文的效率,也能帮助学生有效提高英语写作能力。批改网能指出作文每一句中存在的拼写、语法、词汇、搭配错误,并一一给出修改建议。此外,批改网还能为学生提供特定知识点的扩展训练、搭配推荐、参考例句等,帮助学生自主学习。

2. iWrite英语写作教学与评阅系统(https://iwrite.unipus.cn/)

iWrite英语写作教学与评阅系统与国内外各大考试写作标准接轨,为学习者的文章提供基于语言、内容、篇章结构及技术规范四个维度的智能批改服务,批改和评分的人机相关性系数达0.9以上。该系统可以做到机器智能自动评阅作文,提供写作语料库供学习者自主学习,开展线上、线下混合式教学,将机器评价、同伴互评、教师评价相结合,通过大数据了解不同学习者的写作习惯,并给出具有针对性的建议。

3. 1Checker(http://www.1checker.com/)

1Checker(易改)是一款由杭州硅易科技有限公司[后更名为校宝在线(杭州)科技股份有限公司]自主研发,基于云计算的英语写作辅助软件。1Checker功能强大,不仅能够帮助学习者发现并改正各种英语文本中的错误,而且能提供润色建议,提升文章的质量。无论是学生、教师还是职场人士,都可以通过使用1Checker来提升自己的英语写作水平。1Checker专门针对中国英语学习者常见的错误类别开发了专门的纠错机制,包括冠词错误、名词单复数错误、介词错误、专有名词大小写错误、词性错误、缺少be动词、主谓一致错误、代词错误、时态错误、形容词语序错误等。它还能发现一些常用文字处理软件无法定位的拼写和语法错误。除了纠错外,1Checker还提供润色建议,帮助学习者优化表达,提升文章的质量。对于已经检测出的错误,1Checker会提供详细的解释和修改建议,帮助学习者快速理解并改正错误。它还有内置词典功能,学习者可以随时查找单词的释义和用法。

4. 冰果英语智能作文评阅系统(http://writing.bingoenglish.com/www/index.php/welcome)

冰果英语智能作文评阅系统是一款功能强大、准确率高、易于使用的英语作文评阅系统。它不仅能够帮助学生提高英语写作水平,而且能够辅助教师进行教学管理和教学改进。它基于人工智能技术,能够自动评阅英语作文,帮助学生更好地掌握英语写作技巧,提高英语写作水平。系统从词汇、语法、文风、内容等多个维度为作文给出综合评分,为学生提供客观的写作评价。在评阅期间,系统还可以实时给出修改建议,帮助学生及时发现并改正错误。依照学生的写作水平和需求,系统可以推荐相应的学习资源,帮助学生扬长避短,提升写作能力。

5. Purdue OWL(http://owl.englishpurdue.eduhandouts/pw)

Purdue OWL(Online Writing Lab)是由普渡大学文学院开发的网站,为学生、教育工作者以及希望提升英文写作技能的人提供了宝贵的工具和资源。通过该网站,学习者可以了解专业的写作技巧和方法,提高自己的写作能力和水平。同时,该网站的引文生成器和在线社区也能为学习者提供便利和支持。

6. WhiteSmoke Just Write(http://www.whitesmoke.com/)

这是一款功能强大、操作简便的英语写作学习网站,能为学习者提供写作润色建议,并提供翻译服务。此外,该网站还具有高级语法检查、写作风格检查、智能降低重复率等功能。无论是学生、教师还是职场人士,都可以通过使用它来提升自己的英语写作水平。

7. ETS Criterion(http://criterion.ets.org)

ETS Criterion是由美国ETS测试中心开发的作文自动评价系统,该系统是一款基于网络的教学写作工具,帮助学习者在即时诊断反馈和标准分数的指导下构思、撰写和修改自己的作文,能帮助学生按照自己的节奏练习写作,得到即时的反馈,并根据反馈修改文章,还能帮助教师减少作文的批改量,腾出时间来专注于学生的作文内容和教授更高水平的写作技巧。

8. NoodleTools(http://noodletools.com)

NoodleTools是由美国NoodleTools公司开发的在线写作辅助系统,专门为学校和研究机构设计,旨在帮助学生和教师更有效地进行研究和写作。该系统集成了文献搜索、笔记整理、引文生成等多种功能,是一个内容全面的在线写作和研究平台。系统界面友好,易于操作,适合各年龄段的用户。

9. WordNet(http://wordnet.princeton.edu)

WordNet是在普林斯顿大学心理学教授乔治·A.米勒的指导下建立和维护的、基于认知语言学的英语词典,提供英语词汇的语义信息,包括词义、同义词、反义词、上下位关系等。WordNet在学术研究、自然语言处理和教育学习等领域都有广泛的应用前景。通过Word-Net,用户可以更深入地理解英语单词的含义和用法,提高语言处理的准确性和效率。

10. Hemingway Editor(http://www.hemingwayapp.com/)

Hemingway Editor是一款非常实用的文案修改工具,能够帮助学习者提升文本的可读性。无论是专业写手还是普通用户,都能从中受益并获得更好的写作体验。Hemingway Editor通过分析句子结构、词汇难度等指标,为学习者提供清晰、简洁的写作建议。该工具还能检测文本的阅读难度,并依据难度等级给出改进建议。Hemingway Editor通过调整句子结构、替换复杂词汇来降低文本的阅读难度,使其更加易于理解。它具备强大的纠错功能,能够检测拼写错误、语法错误,并提供修改建议。Hemingway Editor适合各类写作场景,能为学术论文、新闻报道、商务信函的写作等提供有效的帮助。

11. grammarly(https://www.grammarly.com/)

grammarly是一款集英语语法检查、拼写检查、风格改善、抄袭检测等多项功能为一体的英语写作辅助工具。它能够自动检查并纠正英文文章中的语法错误,如主谓不一致、单复数使用不当、固定短语搭配错误、动词时态错误等;能自动检查并纠正拼写错误的单词,并提供正确的备选单词;可以根据文章内容自动指出标点符号使用不当的问题,帮助学习者及时修改;提供同义词建议,避免多次使用同一个英文单词,使表达更加自然流畅;能够纠正不恰当的文体风格,并给出整体风格建议。grammarly支持Windows、Mac、iOS、iPad和Android等多个平台,用户可以在网页、浏览器插件、桌面应用、Microsoft Word等多个场景中使用grammarly进行写作和修改。它是一款功能强大、易于使用的英语写作辅助工具,能够帮助用户提升英语写作的质量、准确性和可读性。无论是学生、教师、职场人士,还是翻译工作者,都能从grammarly中受益。

12. AutoCrit(www.autocrit.com)

AutoCrit是一款专为提升写作质量而设计的专业写作分析工具。AutoCrit能够对文章的风格和语气进行深度分析,帮助学习者识别并改进文章中的潜在问题。它能够检测文本中的语法错误、拼写错误以及标点使用不当等问题,并提供相应的修正建议;能够通过对写作目的和风格的分析,生成个性化的改进建议,学习者可以根据自己的写作需求,获得更加精准的反馈。该工具支持从语法、结构、词汇等多个维度对文章进行评分,全面评估学习者的写作水平。这种多维度的评分方式有助于学习者更全面地了解自己的写作水平,并找到提升的方向。AutoCrit还提供错误检测和修正建议,针对文章的流畅度、表达效果等提出优化建议,帮助学习者提升文章的整体质量和可读性。

13. PaperRater(http://www.paperrater.com/free_paper_grader)

PaperRater是一款功能强大、专业性强、用户体验好的在线论文检测及校对工具。它不仅能够帮助用户检查文档中的拼写、语法和抄袭问题,而且具有写作建议和自动评分等功能。对于需要撰写论文或进行学术研究的用户来说,PaperRater是一个不可或缺的工具。PaperRater能够检查文档中的拼写和语法错误,并提供详细的修改建议;能帮助用户改进写作风格和表达,识别并纠正错误的措辞、冗长的句子、笨拙的结构等问题;具备强大的抄袭检测能力,能够检测文章中的抄袭内容。PaperRater拥有自动评分系统,能根据文章的质量给出评分。

14. SpellCheckPlus(http://spellcheckplus.com/)

SpellCheckPlus是一个在线的修正英语语法和英语句子拼写错误的网站,它支持包括英语在内的多种语言。SpellCheckPlus功能强大,易于使用,能够帮助用户快速准确地检查文本中的错误,并提供修改建议,从而提高文本的质量。SpellCheckPlus能够检查文本中的拼写错误,并提供正确的拼写建议,具备语法检查功能,能够识别并纠正句子中的语法错误。

特别值得一提的是，SpellCheckPlus能够检测到英语非母语的外国学生经常犯的错误。无论是学生、教师还是专业从事写作的人士，都可以从这款工具中受益。

15. ProWritingAid（https://prowritingaid.com/）

ProWritingAid由Orpheus Technology公司开发，它的语法检查功能十分强大，分类比较细致，既可以检查拼写错误，还能检查用词是否老套累赘，语言风格是否过于口语化，句子和段落长度是否合适，有无抄袭等问题。它旨在帮助用户提升写作技能，无论是学术论文、小说还是商业报告，都能通过这款工具得到有效的改进。

四、常见的英语词典

1. 牛津英语词典（https://languages.oup.com/products/dictionary-solutions/）

牛津英语词典是由英国牛津大学出版社出版的英语词典，被誉为最权威的英语词典之一。牛津英语词典拥有超过40万个精确词条，包括乔叟、莎士比亚等著名作家使用过的罕见词。牛津英语词典提供词源分析以及不同地方英语的拼写差异，涵盖了所有英语国家的地方英语，包括北美、南非、澳大利亚、新西兰和加勒比等。每个词条都附有丰富的引证例句，帮助读者理解词汇在不同语境中的用法。全部发音使用国际音标标注，方便读者准确发音。牛津英语词典因其严谨的编纂态度、广泛的收词范围和丰富的例句资源，成为英语词汇研究的重要工具，具有极高的学术价值。对于英语学习者、研究者以及翻译工作者来说，牛津英语词典是不可或缺的参考书。牛津英语词典是英语词汇研究领域的经典之作，其权威性和实用性得到了广泛的认可。

2. 剑桥词典（https://dictionary.cambridge.org）

剑桥词典是由英国剑桥大学出版社出版的词典，以其权威性、科学性和实用性在英语学习者中享有盛誉。剑桥词典以庞大的剑桥英语语料库（Cambridge English Corpus）和剑桥学习者语料库（Cambridge Learner Corpus）为基础，不仅涵盖英国英语，而且兼顾美国英语、澳大利亚英语等世界其他地区的英语，是名副其实的"国际英语词典"。剑桥词典提供多种词典类型选择，包括英语词典、学习词典、基础英式英语词典和基础美式英语词典等，满足不同学习者的需求。词典中的词汇释义详尽，包括词性、音标、单复数、英英释义、例句等，并标注了词汇在欧洲共同语言参考标准（Common European Framework of Reference for Languages，CEFR）中的等级，帮助学习者了解词汇的难易程度。剑桥词典还支持多种语言切换，共有16种语言可供选择，满足全球学习者的需求。剑桥词典以其庞大的语料库支持、国际化的视角、丰富的内容和便捷的功能，在英语学习者中赢得了广泛赞誉。无论是纸质词典还是在线词典，都是英语学习者不可或缺的工具。

3. 柯林斯英语词典（https://www.collinsdictionary.com/）

柯林斯英语词典是由英国第二大图书出版集团哈珀·柯林斯出版的。柯林斯英语词典最早出版于1979年。柯林斯英语词典以实用、全面、现代化著称，已经成为全球范围内英语学习者的良师益友，它不仅收录了大量的词汇、词组和释义，而且不断更新和增补，以适应语言发展的需求。词典收录了超过11万个英语词汇、短语,注重对英语词汇的释义和用法进行详尽说明,提供语法和发音方面的指南,帮助学习者更好地掌握英语。其编写依据是世界著名的三大语料库之一——The Bank of English 语料库。柯林斯英语词典以例句解释为主,这些例句均由最简明的用词构成,即使只有较低水平词汇基础的读者也能轻松看懂词典。同时,例词和例句均取材于实际语料库,确保了语言的鲜活和地道。

4. 韦氏词典(https://www.merriam-webster.com/)

韦氏词典是由美国出版公司梅里亚姆-韦伯斯特公司出版的英语词典,它是美国英语词典的代表作之一。韦氏词典最早可以追溯到1828年,至今已有近两个世纪的历史。韦氏词典收录了大量的词汇、词组和释义,内容详尽,不仅提供词汇的释义和用法,而且有语法和发音方面的指南,非常适合英语学习者使用。韦氏词典特别关注美国英语的专业性和全面性,因其详细、实用和权威的特点而受到广泛好评,在美国以及北美洲地区特别受欢迎,是英语学习者和专业人士的必备工具之一。

References

[1] Shirley Taylor.商务英语写作实例精解[M].7版.卢艳春,白荣梅,译.北京:外语教学与研究出版社,2014.

[2] 禹海玲.高等学校英语应用能力考试模拟试题集[M].北京:机械工业出版社,2006.

[3] 常红梅.新世纪英语写作教程[M].北京:北京大学出版社,2009.

[4] 晨梅梅.实用写作教程[M].上海:上海外语教育出版社,2008.

[5] 崔文凯,王琰.商务文书写作一本通[M].北京:中国言实出版社,2005.

[6] 丁往道,吴冰,钟美荪,等.英语写作手册[M].北京:外语教学与研究出版社,2010.

[7] 方有林.商务应用文写作[M].上海:同济大学出版社,2010.

[8] 冯修文.文秘英语实训[M].3版.北京:中国人民大学出版社,2019.

[9] 管春林.国际商务英语写作[M].杭州:浙江大学出版社,2006.

[10] 何光明.新国际商务英语写作(中级)[M].上海:上海教育出版社,2005.

[11] 何维湘.商务英语应用文写作[M].广州:中山大学出版社,1997.

[12] 胡英坤,车丽娟.商务英语写作[M].北京:外语教学与研究出版社,2013.

[13] 胡仲文,吴祯福.实用英语写作[M].北京:外语教学与研究出版社,1997.

[14] 金双玉,钦寅.外贸英语:函电与单证[M].上海:同济大学出版社,2006.

[15] 李健.实用英语写作[M].北京:外语教学与研究出版社,2011.

[16] 廖瑛.实用英语应用文写作[M].长沙:中南大学出版社,2004.

[17] 刘礼进.实用英文写作[M].2版.广州:中山大学出版社,2003.

[18] 刘庆秋.商务英语应用文写作辅导用书[M].北京:对外经济贸易大学出版社,2010.

[19] 戚云方.新编外经贸英语函电与谈判[M].杭州:浙江大学出版社,2002.

[20] 施晓燕,李红.商务英语应用文写作[M].北京:科学出版社,2010.

[21] 束光辉.新编商务英语写作教程[M].北京:清华大学出版社,北京交通大学出版社,2007.

[22] 王朝晖.实用外贸英语谈判与函电[M].北京:对外经贸大学出版社,2006.

[23] 王妍,刘亚卓.外贸函电[M].北京:北京大学出版社,2013.

[24] 吴柏祥,黄静茹,李清辉,等.商务英语写作[M].北京:清华大学出版社,北京交通大学出版社,2005.

[25] 吴寒,刘子毅.实用英语应用写作[M].广州:中山大学出版社,2003.

[26] 徐云珠.英汉旅游应用文手册[M].北京:汉语大词典出版社,2006.

[27] 杨国俊,邱革加.商务英语读写教程[M].北京:北京航空航天大学出版社,2003.

[28] 张莉,连晓丽.商务英语写作[M].北京:经济管理出版社,2006.

[29] 张玉娟,陈春田,邹云敏,等.新世纪实用英语写作[M].3版.北京:外语教学与研究出版社,2013.